Improving Literacy Instruction With Classroom Research

To the memory of my mother, Marguerite M. Deeney,
who considered teaching the greatest profession.

Improving Literacy Instruction With Classroom Research

Theresa A. Deeney

CORWIN PRESS
A SAGE Company

For information:

Corwin Press
A SAGE Company
2455 Teller Road
Thousand Oaks, California 91320
www.corwinpress.com

SAGE Ltd.
1 Oliver's Yard
55 City Road
London, EC1Y 1SP
United Kingdom

SAGE India Pvt. Ltd.
B 1/I 1 Mohan Cooperative
  Industrial Area
Mathura Road, New Delhi 110 044
India

SAGE Asia-Pacific Pte. Ltd.
33 Pekin Street #02-01
Far East Square
Singapore 048763

Printed in the United States of America

Library of Congress Cataloging-in-Publication Data

Deeney, Theresa A.
  Improving literacy instruction with classroom research / Theresa A. Deeney.
    p. cm.
  Includes bibliographical references and index.
  ISBN 978-1-4129-4088-7 (cloth)—ISBN 978-1-4129-4089-4 (pbk.)
  1. Reading—Research.   2. Literacy.   I. Title.

  LB1050.6.D44 2009
  428.4072—dc22   2008025416

This book is printed on acid-free paper.

08   09   10   11   12   10   9   8   7   6   5   4   3   2   1

Acquisitions Editor:	Cathy Hernandez
Editorial Assistants:	Ena Rosen and Sarah Bartlett
Production Editor:	Appingo Publishing Services
Cover Designer:	Lisa Riley

Contents

Preface

When working in schools and districts, I often hear that teachers are resistant to change. This is odd to me, as teachers are constantly changing and adapting within the classroom. Richardson (1990) points out that change in practice is often construed as teachers doing things *others want them to do*. In this definition, teachers who question certain changes, sometimes top-down changes, are considered resistant to change. This book is about examining and changing literacy teaching practices through reflection and systematic inquiry. It is about teachers being the catalyst for their own change, rather than the recipient of others' ideas for change.

Reflection is the key to change and to effective professional development (Anders, Hoffman, & Duffy, 2000). Teachers continually think back about their teaching and how their actions shaped student learning. This *reflecting-on-action* (Schon, 1987) shapes future teaching; it is a powerful tool for change. Teachers also *reflect-in-action* (Schon, 1987). As they teach, they continually question themselves and adjust what they are doing "on the spot." The intertwining of reflection-in-action and reflection-on-action, *reciprocal reflection-in-action* (Schon, 1983)—the ability to stop and think, adjust and evaluate, and look back to reframe, rethink, and react—is necessary for change in the uncertain and complex reality of teaching. It is also the frame for this book.

As a literacy teacher educator, I puzzle through how to examine my own teaching practices to learn about myself, make changes, and determine how what I do impacts the knowledge and practice of teachers. I develop tasks and activities, gather information about how teachers use them and what they think of them, and make decisions about where to go from there. After several years of systematically putting into place and examining tools to help teachers reflect on, examine, and change their classroom literacy practices, and evaluate their effect on students' learning, I am convinced that classroom research is one of the most valuable tools for accomplishing this.

Although there are many names for teachers doing research on their own practice within their own classrooms (*action research, teacher inquiry, classroom research, classroom study, teacher research*), I like Cochran-Smith and Lytle's (1999) definition of *teacher research*:

> We use the term *teacher research* here in the broadest possible sense to encompass all forms of practitioner inquiry that involve systematic, intentional, and self-critical inquiry about one's work in K–12, higher education, or continuing education classrooms, schools, programs, and other formal educational settings. This definition includes inquiries that others may refer to as action research, practitioner inquiry, teacher or teacher educator self-study, and so on, but does not necessarily include reflection or other terms that refer to being thoughtful about one's educational work in ways that are not necessarily systematic or intentional. (p. 22)

What competent teachers need to know is embedded in their practice, in their reflections on their practice, and in their inquiries about their everyday work (Cochran-Smith & Lytle, 1999, p. 19). Teacher research is meant to answer teachers' problems and questions that arise in practice. At the heart of teacher research is reflection on practice, challenging assumptions, and change.

This is a book about classroom research, but it is equally about literacy teaching and learning. One of my goals in writing this book is to provide information about how to conduct classroom research that leads to teacher, student, and school growth. You will learn how to use classroom research to examine, change, and evaluate your classroom and school practices. You can apply the basic tenets of classroom research to any problem in teaching and learning. My goal is to help you accomplish two things with respect to literacy teaching and learning—first, to see how the reciprocal cycle of classroom research plays itself out in classroom literacy instruction, and second, to learn about research-based literacy practices that other teachers have found successful. You will learn from teachers who have engaged in the process of classroom research in literacy. Teachers, literacy specialists, coaches, and school administrators can use this book to learn the steps of classroom research and learn through colleagues how to design classroom research that is accessible, pragmatic, and important to literacy teaching and learning.

You can use this book in several ways. First, you can use it as a classroom research primer. This book contains guidelines, charts, tables, and information to help you get started with classroom research. Second, you can use this book to learn about specific issues in the core areas of literacy teaching and learning (phonemic awareness, phonics, fluency, vocabulary, and comprehension) and find out what has worked for other teachers. Third, you can use the teachers' research presented in this book as lesson plans or outlines to embark on these projects on your own.

This text is a dual approach to teaching classroom research. In Part I, you will read an overview of the classroom research process. In Part II, you will experience actual research from teachers in the field. These case studies link the theory and process chapters of Part I to classroom application. This text is based on sound theoretical and research-based perspectives. The classroom research framework originally outlined by Lewin (1948) has been adapted and refined. The idea of using classroom research as a tool for reflection and changing practice is well established (Darling-Hammond, 1996; Dinkelman, 1997; Gray-Schlegel & Matanzo, 1993; Hensen, 1996), as is the practice of using case studies for teaching and learning the process and product of classroom research (Yin, 2003).

Part I of this book, Understanding Classroom Research, presents the step-by-step process of classroom research and contextualizes it through literacy teaching and learning. Chapter 1 describes the background of classroom research and presents the steps necessary to accomplish it. Chapter 2 highlights the recursive nature of classroom research through vignettes of teachers' research process. Chapter 3 focuses on choosing the most appropriate way to analyze data collected throughout the research.

In the current climate of federal mandates, reports, and funding streams such as No Child Left Behind, the Report of the National Reading Panel (2000), and Reading First, researchers, teachers, and school professionals are focusing much attention on five core areas of reading: phonemic awareness, phonics, fluency, vocabulary, and comprehension. You will read about classroom research in each of these areas in this book. Within these, there is virtually an endless supply of issues to watch for and notice in a classroom.

Part II, Teachers' Classroom Research in Literacy, presents research conducted by teachers. The first section, Looking at Teaching Within Mandated Programs, includes three chapters that describe how teachers explored their own teaching practices within the reality of district or school mandates. Oftentimes teachers are required to implement literacy programs or administer assessments that they do not find effective. Systematically gathering data can help teachers adjust instruction and inform supervisors or administrators of what is or is not working. In Chapter 4, Maureen, a K–1 teacher, analyzed how her teaching practice through the basal reader was or was not facilitating students' understanding of text and participation in text discussions. Maureen uses transcript analysis to view her read-aloud practice and analyze her role as a discussion facilitator. Chapter 5 focuses on assessment. We know that the purpose of assessment is to inform instruction. Yet, with accountability pressures, teachers are finding it difficult to keep up with the sheer volume of data. In this chapter, Jessica describes how she incorporated district-mandated assessments, filled in the holes in her assessment data, and developed a system to pull the data together to inform instruction. Chapter 6 focuses on differentiating instruction. Teachers, particularly teachers of beginning readers, are often told to differentiate instruction, yet at the same time are handed a specific program to use for all students. How does a teacher reconcile these mixed messages and provide students with differentiated instruction appropriate to their developmental levels? In this chapter, Jenn, a first-grade teacher, describes how she planned a differentiated program of word study instruction by first assessing her students, then integrating the district-required program with thoughtfully-chosen supplemental programs to help all learners.

The second section of Part II, Tying Research to Practice, presents four chapters illustrating how teachers have turned research-based ideas into practice. In Chapter 7, Jayne, a second-grade teacher, describes planning and implementing structured vocabulary instruction in her classroom. Chapter 8 highlights fluency. Ruth Lynn discusses her research into helping her students achieve greater reading fluency, and teaching them about themselves as both readers and listeners. Chapter 9 presents phonemic awareness. In this chapter, Joell, a middle school special education teacher, talks about how she found out that her struggling readers lacked these skills and how she developed and assessed a program to teach them. Chapter 10 features vocabulary. We know from research that vocabulary is crucial to success in reading. We also know that middle school-age students can be tough to involve in learning. This chapter focuses on how two teachers, Sandy and Angela, developed similar projects to enhance middle schoolers' vocabulary learning through teaching Greek and Latin roots.

Each teacher research chapter features spotlights to highlight a part of the classroom research cycle that is particularly well represented in the research and a specific literacy area (vocabulary, phonemic awareness, fluency) or practice (differentiating instruction, keeping track of data). Annotations guide the reader through the cases by connecting ideas from the overview chapters to the process as it unfolds within the teachers' research. Each chapter in Part II ends with a wrap-up of concepts and suggested tasks that focus on both the classroom research process and ideas in literacy teaching and learning to help you apply both to your own classroom teaching.

This book would not be complete without a discussion of ethics in research, found in Chapter 11. Most of you will be conducting research to improve your own teaching rather than to present or publish your findings. Regardless, understanding your responsibility as a researcher to your research participants and their families is always a top priority.

Acknowledgments

I am fortunate to work with outstanding teachers who exemplify what it means to be reflective practitioners. I am deeply grateful to those who share their research in this book: Joell Aristi, Ruth Lynn Butler, Angela Christina, Kerri Fairbanks, Jessica Lavallee, Jennifer Limoges, Sandra Lovejoy, Stephanie Rezendes, Maureen Sullivan, Gail Tella, and Jayne Ward. Although I am helping to tell their stories, the work is theirs.

Much of my own learning comes from other teachers. My mother-in-law, Dolores I. Zapata de Amante, taught fifty years in public schools, mostly in bilingual classrooms. Her experiences helped me understand the effects of "English only" legislation. My graduate students teach me each day. I learn from them how they approach teaching, how they learn about teaching, and how they think about teaching. Their insights help me refine my own practices. I am grateful to Lisa Hochwarter and Tricia Milburn for allowing me to quote excerpts from their discussions of central issues in their teaching.

I owe a debt of thanks to Cathy Hernandez, my editor at Corwin Press, and to her team of reviewers whose suggestions for revisions helped me refine my ideas and my writing. I am also grateful to Ena Rosen, editorial assistant at Corwin Press, and to Lisa Allen and Belinda Thresher at Appingo Publishing Services, who managed the many details of bringing a work to press.

My large, boisterous family, "the loud family," has nurtured me with love, camaraderie, and intellectual stimulation. Each member, blood or water, in-law or out-law, has taught me a great deal. My sister, Carole Redden, the quietest member, was my first teacher. She taught me to read, and instilled in me a love of learning. From the time I began to talk, she began patiently answering my constant questions.

I am thankful each and every day for the love and support of my own incredible family. My children, Christian and Olivia, have taught me lessons about life, both personal and professional. From them, I have gained a keener sense of children, literacy learning, and school from the other side of the desk. As a teacher, administrator, and reading specialist, I only thought I knew these. I am humbled now by what I did not know, and hope that I am more understanding as I work with children and families. My husband, Joseph Amante, shows me life from a different perspective. He sees in ways I do not, approaches things as I do not, and has helped me realize that my way is not the only way.

PUBLISHER'S ACKNOWLEDGMENTS

Corwin Press gratefully acknowledges the contributions of the following reviewers:

Wendy Allen
Language Arts Teacher
Mid-Prairie Middle School
Kalona, IA

Carol Gallegos
Literacy Coach
Hanford Elementary School District
Hanford, CA

Debbie Halcomb
Teacher
R. W. Combs Elementary School
Happy, KY

Jude Huntz
English Teacher
The Barstow School
Kansas City, MO

Laura Linde
K–5 Literacy Coach
Hoover Elementary
North Mankato, MN

Terri Lurkins
Reading Specialist
Highland Middle School
Highland, IL

Michael Putman
Assistant Professor of
    Elementary Education
Ball State University
Muncie, IN

Patrick A. Roberts
Assistant Professor of Educational
    Foundations and Inquiry
Director of the Curriculum and
    Social Inquiry Doctoral Program
National-Louis University
Evanston, IL

Roselyne Thomas
Literacy Coach
Dutch Fork Middle School
Irmo, SC

About the Author

Theresa A. Deeney is Associate Professor of reading education and coordinator of the graduate reading program at the University of Rhode Island. After finishing her own teacher preparation in elementary and special education, she began her career as a special education teacher. She then went on to receive her MEd in educational administration, and served as a school principal. For over twenty years, her roles included teacher, principal, reading specialist, and consultant in urban schools in Massachusetts, New Hampshire, and California. Prior to her appointment at the University of Rhode Island, she coordinated a large-scale research project at Boston University and at the Center for Reading and Language Research at Tufts University. She taught graduate courses in reading at Lesley College, Harvard Graduate School of Education, and Boston College. In 1997, she received her EdD in reading, language, and learning disabilities from the Harvard Graduate School of Education. She currently works closely with teachers on classroom research and inquiry practices that further their own professional development, and has forged school district/university partnerships focused on teacher professional development. In 2007, she received the Outstanding Outreach award from the College of Human Science and Services at the University of Rhode Island for her work with urban teachers. Her research and teaching focus on teacher education and reflective teaching practices, including classroom research. She lives in South Kingstown, Rhode Island, with her husband and two school-age children.

PART I

Understanding Classroom Research

1

What Is Classroom Research?

Kurt Lewin (1948) pioneered the concept that regular people, not "scientists" or "researchers," can systematically notice things going on around them, reflect on them, and make plans to change them. Lewin called this *action research*. In the years since Lewin coined the term *action research*, many other labels have been used for research done by teachers and school professionals. I like the term *teacher research* and Lytle and Cochran-Smith's definition of *teacher research* as "systematic, intentional inquiry by teachers about their own school and classroom work" (1990, p. 84). However, I do not want people to think that this book and these ideas are strictly for teachers. Therefore, I choose to use the term *classroom research* throughout this book, emphasizing that Lytle and Cochran-Smith's definition of *teacher research* includes professionals other than teachers—such as literacy coaches, reading specialists, instructional coaches, special education teachers, and others who work in classrooms with teachers and students. My adaptation of Lytle and Cochran-Smith's definition follows.

Classroom research is "systematic, intentional inquiry by teachers and other school/classroom professionals about their own school and classroom work."

Classroom research is a cyclical process. Schon (1983), in his discussion of reflection, talks about problematizing, acting, and reacting. In its simplest form, these ideas represent the cycle of classroom research. Classroom research is about reflecting, acting, and reacting. It is about thinking through what you see, taking steps to change practice and learning, thinking about those steps, and taking more steps.

THE STEPS OF CLASSROOM RESEARCH

Classroom research begins with noticing, observing, or identifying something in the classroom—something that you wonder about. Perhaps it is an aspect of teaching and learning that could be going better. This noticing then leads to finding out more, which leads to a more specific question. Once you identify the question, you set out to answer it. You plan what to do, carry out the plan, gather data, reflect on what those data mean, and decide once again on what to do. This cyclical process is reflected in Figure 1.1.

Figure 1.1 The Recursive Steps of Classroom Research

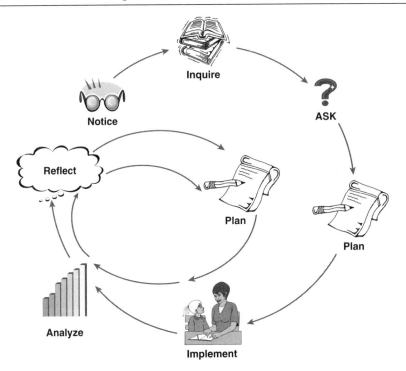

Let us take a look at this process in more detail.

Step 1: Notice. Observe what's going on in your classroom.

The important aspect of Step 1 in the classroom research cycle is to be a good observer—to *see* what you and your students are doing. When observing and noticing your classroom, zero in on something that you struggle with as a teacher and that students struggle with as learners.

Try keeping a journal to help you think about what goes on in your classroom and to identify areas of need. Your journal does not need to be formal;

it is a place for you to write down observations of your teaching and your students' participation in your instruction and activities. If you already have an idea for an area of focus, you can concentrate your journal entries on that area of your practice. If not, you might find it helpful to jot down notes about each segment of your instruction. What were you doing and saying? How did students act or react? How did you know students "got" what they were doing? What did students struggle with? As you jot down your observations, also note potential questions to answer in research. You will not identify your specific question here, but identifying some initial thoughts will help you with the rest of the process. For example, you may notice that not all of your students are catching on to something that you are teaching. There are a few questions in that observation: Is this the right program for my students? Am I structuring this instruction so the students can understand? Am I in my students' Zone of Proximal Development (Vygotsky, 1978)? The checklist in Table 1.1 might help you think about noticing things in your classroom.

Literacy teaching is complex and multifaceted. Teachers usually have no trouble identifying literacy issue*s* (plural) they need to investigate; identifying *one* literacy issue proves challenging. In Table 1.2 teachers share some of the issues they have noticed in core areas of literacy identified in the National Reading Panel Report (2000). The ones with an asterisk (*) are included in Part II of this book.

Although the five core areas are critical for practice, they are not the only areas of literacy instruction or investigation. Both students and teachers struggle with students' motivation to read, engagement in reading, and second-language issues; young children may have difficulty with concepts about print, the language of storybooks, and early writing skills; and teachers might struggle with organizational practices or reconciling district mandates with the struggles and progress of their students. These are all possible topics for classroom research. In Table 1.3, teachers share other issues they have noticed in their classrooms.

Step 2: Inquire. Learn about your focus area.

Traditional researchers begin with a review of theory and relevant research in their area of interest. As a teacher conducting classroom research, you should do the same so that you understand *what* you are noticing, *why* it is important to students' education, and *how* it relates to instruction. Whether you formally write about your classroom research or not, you should be able to explain to yourself and others how the research you want to conduct fits within your given area. Researching your area of interest will help you focus on one or two questions and will generate ideas to implement with your students. Figure 1.2 shows a staircase as an example of how to think about moving systematically from your classroom observation through theory and research to practical application. Think of creating a set of guiding principles that lead you from research and theory, to what has been shown in practice, and then to what you want to figure out.

Table 1.1 Questions to Ask When Observing Your Teaching and Students' Learning

How to start:

- Begin by writing down what you notice going on in your classroom. Unless you already have an instructional topic on which you want to zero in, jot down notes about each area of instruction (each subject you teach).

- After a week or two, go back through your notes in each subject area.

Questions to ask first:

- What do I mean to teach? (Make some notes about your specific goals for each area of your instruction.)

- Am I actually teaching what I think I'm teaching? (Note how you know your instruction matches your goals.)

- Are my students learning? (Note how you know students are learning.)

- Are my students fully engaged? (Note how you know students are engaged.)

Narrow down your observations:

- Think about the answers to the questions above. Choose an area of instruction where your answers are not as positive as you hoped.

Now that you have an area of focus, think about these teacher questions:

- Am I using an instructional approach that matches my goals?

- Am I using an instructional approach that students seem to understand? If not, what are they not understanding and how does that relate to my approach?

- Is my pacing appropriate? (Think about your pace with respect to what students are doing. Are they finishing with time to spare? Are they doing the same thing over and over?)

- Am I clearly communicating what I want to teach?

- Am I using different teaching techniques to capitalize on a variety of student learning styles? What approaches of mine match what learning styles?

- Am I really passionate about my teaching in this area?

Think about these student questions:

- Are my students equally engaged and learning? Are some students engaged, but not others? How do I know all students are engaged and learning?

- What are students doing? How are they doing it?

- What is student progress like in this area? How do I know?

- Where are my students with respect to where they are supposed to be? How do I know?

Table 1.2 Teachers' Observations in the Five Core Areas of Literacy

I notice that:

Phonemic Awareness

- My middle school struggling readers can't get words off the page well or play simple language games (Pig Latin, rhyming games, etc.).*

Phonics/Word Study

- I am not reaching all of my students with my current word study instruction.*
- My students are making better progress in reading than in spelling.
- My bilingual students have trouble spelling due to confusions between Spanish and English.
- My kindergartners are supposed to learn sight words, yet we really haven't been teaching these.

Fluency

- My students are not sounding like "good" readers when they read aloud.*
- My ELL students have fairly good word reading skills, but don't seem to know English syntax well enough to chunk text into meaningful phrases, which seems to affect fluency and comprehension.

Vocabulary

- Vocabulary is such an issue with my students!*
- My students should be able to use word parts to figure out the meanings of words they don't know.*
- Not only is vocabulary an issue in reading/language arts, it's an issue in math.

Comprehension

- My students need to know what questions are really asking.
- My students need to learn comprehension strategies.
- When my students meet in literature circles, they only talk about their own role. There's no real discussion.
- My students really struggle with expository text.
- The literary language in novels is such a struggle for my students!

Note: An asterisk indicates that this question is presented in more detail in another chapter of this book.

Table 1.3 Teachers' Observations of Students in Other Areas of Literacy

I noticed that:

Concepts About Print

- My kindergartners, who had little exposure to print prior to school, aren't grasping the whole idea of Concept of Word.

Choice and Motivation

- My students continually choose books that are either too hard or too easy.

- My adolescents are not engaged in reading at all, but the books we read really don't relate to their lives.

- I'm having trouble finding books that interest my students and that are easy enough for them to read.

- I don't know whether my special needs students participate in literature discussions in their classroom.

Literacy Practices

- My read alouds just don't seem to generate much discussion.*

- I am having trouble keeping track of assessment information*

- My students' idea of "responding" to literature is to write one sentence, "I think that . . ."

Understanding Students and Teachers

- I can't figure out how word reading, vocabulary, and comprehension go together for my ELL students.

- We just began a professional development project, but I'm not sure teachers think they need it.

Engaging Others in Literacy Teaching

- We are not using volunteers well in our school

- We just began a professional development project, but I'm not sure teachers think they need it.

Note: An asterisk indicates that this question is presented in more detail in another chapter of this book.

There are many sources for information about literacy research, teaching, and learning. Although literacy journals typically focus on either research or practice, the research is about practice and the practice is based on research. In Table 1.4 you will find examples of research and practice journals. You can access many research publications on the Internet using a research search engine such as Google Scholar (http://www.googlescholar.com). There are also many Web sites devoted to literacy practice. As you review the literature, keep in mind the staircase of inquiry (Figure 1.2).

Figure 1.2 Staircase of Inquiry

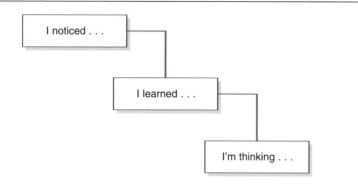

Step 3: Ask. Narrow your area to a specific question.

Once you have gathered information about your topic, you are ready to narrow it down. What do you want to learn? What do you want your students to learn? If your project involves implementing some type of instruction with students, you should have two research questions—one focusing on your teaching, and one focusing on your students' learning. Teacher questions can be logistical, such as, "How can I implement this idea with my students?" They can also focus on process—on looking more deeply at what you are already doing. For example, perhaps you are teaching your students to ask questions that require higher-level thinking. Yet, despite your modeling and scaffolding, they continue to ask basic, retrieval questions. You might decide that you want to look further into your own teaching and ask, "How am I modeling and scaffolding?" or "What am I saying and how does what I say seem to affect how students respond?" The same is true for student learning questions. You might ask a more product-focused question such as, "If I implement my new idea, will students' performance improve?" You might also ask a more process-focused question, such as, "How do my students talk about a particular text?" Look through Table 1.5 to see the questions that came from the other teachers' noticings about the five core areas of literacy teaching and learning.

Classroom Research Question Guide
Teacher-as-Learner Questions:
How is it that I do what I do?
How can I implement this idea?

Student Learning Questions:
If I implement my idea, how will students respond?
How do students do what they do?

Table 1.4 Sources of Research and Practice Information About Literacy

Literacy-Specific Journals	Other Journals That May Contain Literacy Articles
Theory/Research • *Journal of Early Childhood Literacy* • *Journal of Information Literacy (online)* • *Journal of Literacy Research* • *Journal of Literacy and Technology (online)* • *Reading Psychology* • *Reading Research and Instruction* • *Reading Research Quarterly* • *Research in the Teaching of English* • *Reading and Writing Quarterly* • *Scientific Studies in Reading*	**Theory/Research** • *The Elementary School Journal* • *Journal of Scholarship of Teaching and Learning (online)* • *Journal of Teacher Education* • *Journal of Teaching and Learning* • *Learning Disabilities Theory and Practice* • *The Journal of Special Education*
Practice • *English Journal (Middle/HS Language Arts)* • *Journal of Adolescent and Adult Literacy* • *Journal of Reading Education* • *Language Arts* • *Reading Horizons* • *Reading Research and Instruction* • *The Reading Teacher*	**Practice** • *ESL Magazine* • *Intervention in School and Clinic* • *TESOL [Teachers of English to Speakers of Other Languages] Quarterly* • *Teaching and Learning*
Online Practice Resources Literacy Access Online: http://www.literacyaccessonline.com Online Reading Resources: http://www.stewardinc.com Reading A–Z: http://www.readinga-z.com Read-Write-Think: http://www.readwritethink.org Starfall: http://www.starfall.com	

Table 1.5 Questions Based on Teacher Noticings in the Five Core Areas of Reading

Noticings	Teacher Question	Student Question
Phonemic Awareness My middle school struggling readers can't get words off the page well, or play simple language games (Pig Latin, rhyming games, etc.).*	What are the phonics and phonemic awareness skills of my students? If my students struggle with phonics and phonemic awareness, what should I do for instruction?	Will a program of direct instruction in phonological awareness and word study improve my students' reading skills?
Phonics/Word Study I am not reaching all of my students with my current word study instruction.*	How can I design an effective differentiated word study program for my students?	Will the way I have come up with to differentiate my word study instruction help my students make gains in reading?
My bilingual students have trouble spelling due to confusions between Spanish and English.	What are the connections/disconnections between Spanish and English?	Will specifically teaching the connections between Spanish and English orthography combined with the *Words Their Way* program help my students learn and generalize English spelling?
Fluency My ELL students have good word reading skills but don't chunk text into meaningful phrases, which seems to affect fluency and comprehension.	How can I teach my students to use English syntax to chunk text into meaningful phrases?	Will teaching students to chunk text improve their reading fluency and comprehension?
Vocabulary My students should be able to use word parts to figure out the meanings of words.*	How can I design instruction to teach Greek and Latin roots?	Will teaching Greek and Latin roots help students understand the meanings of words they come across in text? Will any improvement in vocabulary help students improve comprehension?

(Continued)

Table 1.5 (Continued)

Vocabulary is also an issue in math.	Can I use children's literature to teach mathematical vocabulary?	Will students be able to use mathematical vocabulary in their writing?
Comprehension My students need to know what questions are really asking.	How can I implement the Question-Answer Relationships (QAR) (Raphael, Highfield, & Au, 2006) procedure with my students?	If I implement QAR, will students' comprehension improve?
My students need to learn comprehension strategies.	How can I implement reciprocal teaching with my students?	How will my students' book discussions change as a result of reciprocal teaching? Will their comprehension improve?
The literary language in novels is such a struggle for my students!	How can I design instruction using sign language to teach students literal versus figurative interpretation?	Will teaching students to talk in pictures using sign language increase their ability to interpret nonliteral text?

Note: An asterisk indicates that this question is presented in more detail in another chapter of this book.

 Step 4: Plan. Make a plan to implement the instruction and collect data.

Planning is a key to classroom research. However, planning is not static. Although you may have set the best plan in place, you might see things that need adjusting or reconceptualizing. Reflecting on what you do and how the students respond will lead you to make changes. Keep the following mantra in mind.

Classroom Research Planning Mantra
Planning is not static.
If I have planned well but things aren't going well, I can change.

Although your research will be dynamic—that is, you will adjust as you go along—you do need to develop an initial plan.

There are three key facets to planning: instruction, logistics, and data collection.

Planning Instruction

To get the most out of your classroom research, you need to make sure you have planned your instruction so that you can put your energy into carrying it out and watching how it unfolds. When planning your instruction, think about the questions in Table 1.6.

Through planning your instruction, you are oftentimes actually answering your teacher-as-learner question. Questions that start with, "How can I . . ." are questions that are initially answered in the planning stage of classroom research. For example, figuring out how you can assist your students in understanding a particular concept begins with investigating what the research says about teaching this concept and then planning how you will teach it. Of course, you might revise your plan as you are engaged in instruction, but you need to select what you want to teach and devise a step-by-step plan for how you will teach it.

Planning Logistics

When thinking about your instruction, plan not only *what* you will implement, but *how* you will implement it. Think about the questions presented in Table 1.7.

Table 1.6 Questions to Help Plan Instruction

• What idea will I teach?	• What is it that I am noticing I want to improve upon myself, or help my students improve upon?
• What kind of instruction will I provide?	• Will I create the instruction myself? • Is there a program already made that I want to use?
• How will I teach it?	• What specific teaching techniques will I use? • How will I explain the concept? What will I say? • How will I model the concept for my students? • How will I have my students engage in guided practice? What will I have my students do? • How will I release responsibility to my students?

(Continued)

Table 1.6 (Continued)

• What materials do I need to have ready?	• What do I need to prepare before I even begin? • What will I need as I go along? • Do I have what I need?
• What pace will I set?	• How long do I project it will it take me to accomplish my goal? • How often should I work with students on this particular instruction? • How will I know when students are ready to move on to the next level of this instruction?

Table 1.7 Questions to Help Plan for Logistics

With whom will I implement my instruction?	Will I work with the whole class? A group of students? Teachers?
What will the structure look like?	Will I do this every day? Will I have some type of routine—a daily or weekly schedule?
Do I need anyone to help me?	Is this something I can do on my own? If not, what resources (people) do I have to help me?
How will I organize my classroom for this instruction?	If I am working in small groups, how much time will I work with each group? What will the other students do during this time? If I am working with someone else, how will I coordinate our schedules? Do I need to change the format of my classroom (for example, do I need to have my students sitting in a different configuration for this instruction)?
Do I need to preteach any organizational structures?	Will I be asking students to follow a new routine, use new materials, or follow new procedures? If so, when and how will I teach these?

Planning Data Collection

One of the hardest parts of classroom research is planning in advance what data you should collect to be able to make some observations about your teaching and your students' learning. If you begin without a clear idea of what data you will collect, you may have lost the opportunity to collect it. Take, for example, a writing project I implemented when I was a reading specialist. Since class size was large (twenty-seven students), and second graders need quite a bit of assistance, one of my teacher-as-learner questions was how to teach students to help one another, to confer with each other and provide some tips, and to talk like writers. This was, in turn, one of my student learning questions, "Will students be able to offer constructive feedback to each other without teacher assistance?" I collected students' writing to understand their process and progress as writers. I taught students to confer with one another and developed tools that would scaffold independence, such as conference forms students completed when they conferred about their writing. I collected these forms for data as well. I thought I had the information I needed to determine whether what the teacher and I were doing in the classroom was working, but this was only partially true.

The writing portfolios were helpful to me in seeing how students' writing was changing over time. However, the conference forms students completed were too superficial for me to understand, and they actually led my conclusions astray about what was going on. However, one day the teacher and I happened to stop long enough to listen to the talk going on around us. These young writers were engaged, listening to each other, giving good feedback, and using writing talk! But I had no record of this transformation, no way to know whether it had been happening slowly all along or whether this was one of those good days in teaching. Because one of my goals was to get students to help one another and talk like writers, in addition to the writing and the writing conference forms, I should have thought to capture the *actual talk* about writing. Looking back, this seems so obvious, but at the time I was so focused on *products* that I didn't consider the *process*, which I will discuss next.

Process Versus Product Data

There are many kinds of data to answer the many kinds of questions you might have about teaching and learning. When you think about the data you should collect, think first about whether you are asking a process or a product question. By *process*, I mean looking at *how* you or your students are doing what you or they are doing. It might be something like the writing project I just described—how students talk about writing. It could also be something like how students' work is changing over time, how students interact with a specific subject, and so on. By *product* questions, I mean questions of whether students have improved in a specific area or what students have learned in a specific area. Table 1.8 presents some examples of process- and product-focused questions and the kinds of data that might answer those questions.

Table 1.8 Research Questions and Types of Data That Answer Them

Product-Focused Question	Product-Focused Data
Will my students' abilities improve if I implement this program?	Results of a specific assessment
Process-Focused Question	**Process-Focused Data**
How are students discussing text?	Video- or audiotape recordings of discussions

You can gather either process- or product-focused data for both teacher-as-learner and student learning questions. Let us look at these in more detail.

Data That Can Answer Student Learning Questions

Test Scores. Test scores are primarily product-focused. From test scores, you can measure what your students have learned (or can demonstrate on a test) about particular concepts. From test scores you might be able to make some inferences about how your teaching has influenced students' understandings of the concepts, but primarily test data will not help you understand *how* students are learning and responding.

Student Artifacts. There are many artifacts you can collect to assess what's going on in the classroom. Additionally, you can use artifacts in a product- or process-focused way. For example, you can use writing samples to determine whether students' scores on a rubric are improving. This is a product-focused view of writing. In other words, you would not necessarily look at *how* the writing was changing or improving, you would simply chart and analyze the rubric scores themselves. However, you could use these same samples to understand *how* student work is changing over time. This is a more process-focused analysis. How are students showing awareness of audience? How are they using literary language?

Rubrics. Although most rubrics are used as product-focused data, they can provide process information. As a product-focused measure, you can use rubric scores to determine whether students have improved in some area. (For example, you can show that your students moved from a score of 2 on a rubric to a score of 4.) You can get at *process* through the design of the rubric itself. Creating a rubric with incremental criteria for the process you want to see unfold can help you capture each student's progress through that process. It does not matter what numerical value you give to the rubric criteria; what matters is what you include as criteria. You will see an example of a product- versus process-focused rubric in Table 1.9.

Table 1.9 Product- and Process-Focused Rubrics

Product-Focused Rubric					
	1	**2**	**3**	**4**	**5**
Uses Writing Mechanics	Does not apply writing mechanics	Applies some writing mechanics	Applies some grade-appropriate writing mechanics	Applies grade-appropriate writing mechanics	Applies advanced writing mechanics
Process-Focused Rubric					
	Exploring Use	**Emerging Use**	**Developing Use**	**Established Use**	**Well-Established Use**
Uses Story Structure to Tell a Complete Story	Writes a simple beginning story (e.g., "I went to my friend's.")	Uses beginning/ middle or beginning/ end structure in a simple narrative (e.g,. "I went to my friend's. We played ball.")	Uses beginning, middle, end structure including character(s), problem, and solution	Uses five elements of story structure in a story (character, setting, problem, events, solution)	Uses five elements of story structure to tell a complete story in which the events lead logically from the problem to the solution
Synthesizes Information in a Research Paper	Presents facts about the topic, but relies on one source of information	Presents information from two sources separately (e.g., writes about information from Source A, then information from Source B, or writes about Topic 1 then Topic 2)	Presents information from two sources by comparing and contrasting the information	Presents information from two sources by comparing and contrasting the information and wraps up information by recapping the facts gained	Presents information from two sources by comparing and contrasting the information and wraps up information by presenting the reader with new information gleaned from the totality of the sources

Surveys, Rating Scales, and Questionnaires. These can help you find out how students respond to given questions or ideas. You can organize survey data as a scale (for example, a Likert scale of 1–5) or as multiple-choice responses. Many surveys have already been created to measure students' attitudes toward school, attitudes toward reading, reading preferences, and other such school-related issues. Most are in the form of a Likert-type scale. The *Elementary Reading Attitude Survey* (McKenna & Kear, 1990), which asks students to respond to questions about reading (e.g., "How do you feel when you read out loud in class?") by circling one of four pictures of the cartoon character Garfield (very happy, a little happy, a little upset, very upset), is a common survey used in schools. The Second Step middle school attitude survey (Committee for Children, http://www.cfchildren.org/ssf/ssevaltoolsf/pdf/mssurvey.pdf) also uses a Likert-type scale ("don't agree" to "completely agree") to try to discover middle school students' attitudes toward school. You can find many informal surveys on the Web, or you can create your own based on what you want to know. Survey, rating scale, and questionnaire data tends to be more product-focused.

Interviews. You can gain a lot of information from talking to students. You can use interviews to gain either product- or process-focused information, depending upon the questions you include in the interview guide. However, interviews are typically designed as process-focused tools to learn what students think about specific topics or areas, or how students perceive that they do what they do.

Video or Audio Recording. Capturing happenings to review at a later time is a wonderful way to figure out what students are doing and how they are doing it. In hindsight, this would have been the ideal type of data for my writing workshop question about students talking and participating as writers.

Data to Answer Teacher-as-Learner Questions

With some classroom research projects you could be collecting data about other teachers (for example, what do teachers think about such-and-such practice). However, for the most part, you will be analyzing your own teaching. There are several ways you can accomplish this, some of which are the same as you might use for student learning questions.

Video or Audio Recording. Video and audio data captures what is happening in the classroom as it is happening. Because what you say and do is captured in real time, you can actually observe yourself "in the moment." Video or audio recordings are powerful data for helping answer questions you might have about *how* you teach or *how* you interact with students. However, they are inherently messier than other forms of data and require careful reflection to analyze.

Research Journal. A research journal is another form of data to help you understand the process of teaching and learning. Keeping a research journal can help you reflect on your day-to-day activities and instruction, and provide the basis for you to understand your teaching and your students' learning. Keeping a journal also helps you supplement your other data so you can better understand and analyze it. For example, Gail, an urban middle school teacher was working with her students on vocabulary. She planned to collect product-focused pre- and post-instruction standardized and informal test data to understand whether students were retaining the vocabulary they were studying, and whether focusing on vocabulary would yield any increase in their formal test scores. However, as she was working with the students, Gail noticed the students noticing words. These students, typically reluctant to participate in class, came up to her to use words and to tell her how they had used words. They raised their hands to use words in class. One student, after asking what *scrawl* meant, replied, "That's a great word. Can you write that down for me? I want to use that word." Maybe Gail's students' standardized test scores will improve, maybe not. But there is another story to be told here, one of awakening students' interest in words and language, which cannot be told through test scores. Keeping an ongoing research journal to record each day's instruction and students' engagement can help tell the untold story.

Choosing data is critical to understanding what you want to understand, so make sure that the data you choose match what you want to know.

Step 5: Implement. Implement the plan and collect data.

Once you have your plan in place, you are ready to implement it and begin collecting data. Keep a binder or some other type of system to store lesson plans, data, and any other research-related artifacts. Some teachers keep their research journal on loose-leaf paper, so they can add it to their binder and keep everything in chronological order.

Remember the classroom research planning mantra: **Planning is not static. If I have planned well, but things aren't going well, I can change.**

As you implement your plan, pay attention to the three planning areas: instruction, logistics, and data collection. You might need to adjust your plan. But do not do so without first reflecting on the data you have gathered thus far. Keep detailed notes in your journal regarding your instruction and students' responsiveness, participation, and understanding.

Instruction

Classroom research is an evolving process. Some teachers find that their instruction flows just fine as planned, others need to adjust their instruction here and there, and still others realize that they asked the wrong question in the first place. This is a valuable learning experience.

Logistics

Although you plan the logistics of your project in advance, you might not anticipate specific problems that will arise. Promptly deal with logistical problems. Identify the problem, stop and think about what is causing it, and revise or reteach the necessary routines.

Data Collection

Hopefully, your plan for data collection can be implemented as planned. But as your project evolves, you may decide to revise the plan. Keep in mind that changing the tool you use to gather *product-focused* data may mean that you are not able to directly compare students' performance from one task to another. For example, let us say that you gave students a particular test at the beginning of the school year, but decided to give a different test at the end of the school year. You might be able to look at both sets of scores and make some statements about student progress, but in all likelihood, the tests are not testing the same exact skills in the same exact way. Before you change the data you collect, make sure you go back to your questions and your original plan and determine if your change will still allow you to answer your questions.

Step 6: Analyze. Analyze and make sense of the data.

Making sense out of data is the beginning of the answer to your research questions. However, your data will only *help* you tell a story; it is up to you to determine what story it is telling. Different kinds of data require different types of analyses. How to analyze different types of data is discussed in more detail in Chapter 3, but some basic tenets of data analysis in classroom research are discussed below.

First, unlike some more formal kinds of research, classroom researchers do not need to wait until an official "end" of their project to analyze their data. Classroom research is meant to inform instruction. It is difficult to inform instruction if that instruction has ended. In classroom research, data analysis is ongoing and recursive. Analysis and reflection on your data will lead you to make changes in your project if needed.

Second, your research journal may be one of the most important sources of data. Your notes about what you are doing and how students are responding will help you decide whether you are on the right course with your project. The best way to begin analysis is to set up an initial timeline for a preliminary or interim analysis of the data that you have collected thus far. Using that, you can reflect (Step 7) to make a plan for where to go from there (Step 8).

Step 7: Reflect. Think about your data and what it means for your instruction.

Reflection is an ongoing part of classroom research. However, I discuss it here as a discrete step to remind you that you need to take time to stop and think. When you are thinking about your interim analysis or a more formal ending analysis, analyzing data can be a tedious process. Sometimes we can get so immersed in it that we lose sight of our questions. We need to remind ourselves to think about what the data mean with respect to teaching, learning, and life in the classroom. It is a time to go back and revisit your original question. What did you want to learn? What do your data tell you about that?

When thinking about your interim analysis, revisit your initial plan for your project in terms of instruction, logistics, and data collection. Are you satisfied that your initial plan is working well in each of these areas? How do you know? Based on this, you may find that you need to make some changes. Here are some questions to guide your thinking as your reflect on your findings thus far:

- Is my project going in the direction I want it to go?
- What do my data tell me about my
  - instruction?
  - logistics?
  - data collection?
- Do I need to make any changes in my plan with respect to instruction, logistics, or data collection?

Step 8: Plan. Follow up by creating an action plan.

Step 8 of the classroom research cycle is a matter of deciding what to do with what you have already done. Action plans range from deciding to adjust something minor in your initial plan to writing up a formal research report. Because classroom research is recursive, you might find that Step 8 really begins another cycle of Steps 4–8. You use the data analysis and reflection to adjust your instruction, continue to gather data, analyze, reflect, and keep cycling through the process.

Deciding to adjust your instruction or logistics or to gather additional data are plans you might make to improve your project as you go. These typically involve planning for yourself and your students. However, let us say, for example, that you are trying to determine how students respond to a new program so you can make some decisions about whether to keep the program. In these cases, your analyses and your action plan might be more formal and involve other people. You may display your data through charts and graphs, think about what those tell you with respect to the program you implemented, and create a plan to present or share the data with other teachers, an administrator, or a committee. Table 1.10 provides some ideas for action plans based on the kinds of research questions you might have and the analyses you may have made.

WRAP UP

In this chapter, you have viewed the eight recursive steps of classroom research. You have seen how other teachers' observations have led them to questions and to choices in what method of data collection might be

Table 1.10 Action Plans

Question	Analysis/Reflection	Action Plan	Type of Plan
If I implement XX, how will my students do on tests?	Students' scores really improved.	Continue with instruction.	Maintain
		Share your project and results with colleagues so they might implement it as well.	Share
		Present data and analysis to administrators for them to consider with respect to curriculum.	Inform
How do I involve my students in instruction?	I'm asking too many questions and not letting students ask and discover on their own.	Develop and implement a plan to release responsibility to students; gather data on your own progress.	Revise
Does my language arts instruction meet the needs of my students?	Some students did really well, others not so well.	Ask another question: How can I structure my instruction to meet the needs of *all* of my students?	Question

appropriate to answer those questions. There is no one "right" question, no one "right" plan, no one "right" piece of data. There is a good deal of "it depends." The take home message here is that classroom research is recursive and ongoing. You need to observe, inquire, ask, and plan to the best of your ability before you begin, but after you begin, carefully observe and analyze. Make changes as you go, but base those changes on data and your analysis of that data.

YOU TRY IT

Trying Out Research.

Begin to think about classroom research that you might want to conduct. Here are some tasks to get you started:

- Focus on Step 1 of the classroom research cycle—notice. Begin keeping a journal in which you jot down things about your instruction and students' learning that puzzle you, frustrate you, intrigue you, or otherwise catch your attention. Do this for a week or two. Then review your notes. Think about this:
  - Are there any common themes that you see?
  - Is there one thing you are writing about more than others?
  - Is there something that is more curious than others?
- Once you have identified one thing (one topic of instruction), go back and try to more carefully "watch" that particular facet of your instruction and students' learning. Take detailed notes and try to focus on what's really happening.

2

Cycling Through the Steps

Until now we have only visited the steps of classroom research linearly from Step 1 through Step 8. You will now meet teachers whose research was not linear—they needed to cycle through the steps. They reflected and made adjustments based on how their research was unfolding. This recursive process is the true nature of classroom research.

STEPHANIE'S RESEARCH

Stephanie is a relatively new teacher in a large urban school who had been moved to another classroom and another grade once again. Although moving from first grade to kindergarten may seem like a small adjustment, Stephanie needed to understand her very emergent readers and the kindergarten curriculum. Rather than beginning by noticing (Step 1) her students' learning within the classroom, Stephanie began by noticing the standards for kindergarten to identify what she was supposed to accomplish. According to her district, kindergartners should be able to recognize fifty sight words by the end of the year. Now Stephanie needed to inquire (Step 2). She found that the district had adopted a list of sight words for each grade, but it did not provide any guidelines about how to teach these words. Many of the resources Stephanie checked talked about teaching sight words in the context of shared reading. Stephanie's teacher and student questions (Step 3) were as follows:

Teacher-as-Learner Question
"How do I embed sight word instruction into shared reading?"

Student Learning Question
"Will my students learn and retain the sight words I teach?"

Stephanie planned (Step 4) to incorporate sight word instruction into her shared reading time, teaching two to three words per week (four-day cycle) using the district's sight word sequence. However, based on her sight word check-ins (Stephanie took individual students aside and asked them to read the words), Stephanie's data showed her (Step 5) that students were not "getting" this embedded instruction.

Step 7: Reflect.

Stephanie felt she was trying to accomplish too much with too little instruction and practice and that she was not targeting the right words.

Stephanie's journal became a major source of reflection on her instruction. She wrote, "When I introduced the words *my* and *your* together this week, the students had a really hard time. I don't know what was going on, but those words seemed too hard for them." She noticed this pattern recurring in her journal. She wrote, "I need to look at the list of words again and see how they are used in my shared reading books." She then cycled back to Step 2 (Inquire) to learn more information about teaching sight words and expectations for kindergartners.

Step 2: Inquire.

Now that Stephanie had a better understanding of her kindergartners' ability to learn the sight words from the instruction she was providing, she was in a position to look differently at sight word instruction in general. She wrote, "After going through the [district] list again and looking at the books we use and how my students responded to instruction, I didn't think the introduction of sight words in our district program was developmentally appropriate. I checked out other lists, and *your* is not a word typically introduced at the beginning of kindergarten. I also don't think my students can handle two to three words per week right now."

Stephanie did not need to ask different questions than those she had originally developed. She moved from Step 2 (Inquire) to her second cycle into planning.

Step 8: Plan.

Stephanie changed her instruction based on her analysis and reflection. She decided to use the pre-primer Dolch word list and introduce one word per four-day cycle. She would then check students' progress in a few weeks. If they did well, she planned to increase instruction to two words per week and then, possibly, three. She also planned to engage students in more practice reading the words. She created several games to put in the literacy center. She also reviewed the words daily using "popcorn words," an idea she found online (http://teachers.net/gazette/AUG03/printable.html#pop). She told students they should know these words so well, they just "pop" out of their mouths. They were delighted to read the words and watch as Stephanie "popped" them out of a popcorn box and threw them on to the floor.

Stephanie's classroom research was not linear. She needed to go back and investigate her topic once she began her research; she also needed to change her plan. However, she continued with her original questions— How can I teach my students sight words? What words should I teach?

You may find that you not only need to change your plans, you may need to rethink your questions. Here is an example of how Kerri, a fourth-grade teacher, did this.

KERRI'S RESEARCH

Kerri noticed (Step 1) that her fourth graders had a particularly hard time responding to inferential questions about what they read, both orally and in writing. After reviewing the research on comprehension (Step 2: Inquire), Kerri found that discussion helps students build understanding of text. Kerri thought that discussion groups might be a helpful tool and that literature journals would provide students with additional practice in responding to text they read. Kerri then investigated models of discussion and discussion groups. She was intrigued by the literature circle model (Daniels, 1994), where students are given roles to participate in a small group discussion (directing the discussion, asking questions, clarifying vocabulary, illustrating text, etc.). Kerri's questions (Step 3) were

---

Teacher-as-Learner Question
"How can I implement literature circles with my students?"

Student Learning Questions
"Will my students show a greater ability to make inferences from text if they participate in literature circles?" and "Will my students' responses to text improve?"

Kerri planned (Step 4) to teach students to engage in literature circles and to have students keep a journal in response to their reading. She planned to tape-record and transcribe discussions and to collect students' literature journals. She was set to implement her plan (Step 5), and she began introducing literature circles and modeled literature journal responses.

Table 2.1 Kerri's First Transcript

Poppy, by Avi	Analysis
T: We have been reading the book, *Poppy,* and you have learned the different roles and jobs for our literature circles. Today you are going to share what you worked on in our literature circle. Let's start with Student 1. [T: OPENS DISCUSSION]	Amount of teacher talk: 34 lines

Amount of student talk: 25 lines

Teacher attempts to link student comments by turning a question back to the group or to the text. She is unsuccessful. Students fail to respond to connection.

Students turning over the current topic to their own role, despite open question on the table.

Inference questions not answered correctly. |
S1: I was the illustrator. I drew a picture of Poppy when Mr. Ocax told them they could not move to a new house. [S-T: ROLE]	
T: Why does the group think that was an important part of the chapter? [T-S: TURN BACK TO S: INFER]	
S3: Maybe because they can't go now. I don't know. [S-T: INCORRECT]	
T: We know that the family needs to move because they have run out of food. Mr. Ocax has told Poppy and her father they cannot move because Poppy and Ragweed went to Bannock Hill without permission. Why is Mr. Ocax telling Poppy and her father they can't move an important part of the chapter? [T: RECAP, T-S: REPEAT Q #1]	
S2: Other mice are mad at Poppy. [S-T: INCORRECT]	
S3: Poppy feels bad. [S-T: INCORRECT]	
S2: I was the connector. [S-T: NR] I connected with this part because I have done some stuff at home and my mom was mad. [NEW ROLE]	
T: What should Poppy do? [T-S: Q #2: INFER/PREDICT]	
S3: [to S2] What did you do to get in trouble? [S-T: NR; S-S: Q: RE S2 CONNECTION, OFF TASK]	
T: When we are in literature circles we need to stick to the book. [T-S: REDIRECT] So, what should Poppy do? Does anyone have any ideas? Let's hear from Student 3. [T-S: REPEAT Q #2]	
S3: I was the questioner. [S-T: NR] My first question is: Why does Poppy have to hold a flag? What will happen to the family? Why does Mr. Ocax say no? [NEW ROLE]	
T: Why do you think Poppy had to hold the flag? [T-S: TURN BACK/INFER]	
S2: So Mr. Ocax would know they were coming. [S-T: CORRECT]	

Poppy, by Avi	Analysis
T: Okay. Anybody else? What does everyone else think? What do we know about when the mice travel in the forest? [T-S: Q: CONNECT/RETRIEVE]	
S4: They need to ask Mr. Ocax. [S-T: CORRECT]	
T: Good! So do we think this was a way to let Mr. Ocax know they were coming for a purpose and not just traveling without permission? [T-S: Q: CONNECT/INFER]	
S: [S-T: NR]	
T: Let's look at the next question. What will happen to the family? We discussed this earlier. Does anyone remember what we talked about? [T-S: REPEAT S: Q]	
S5: They do not have food. [S-T: PARTIALLY CORRECT]	
T: What do we know about why Mr. Ocax said no? [T-S: Q: CONNECT/RETRIEVE]	
S1: They did not ask permission. [S-T: CORRECT]	
T: This brings us back to our earlier question. [T-S: LINK] What should Poppy do, now that she knows Mr. Ocax won't let them move and her family doesn't have enough food to survive? [RECAP] What do you think? What should her plan be? Any ideas? [REPEAT Q #2]	
S4: Well I think maybe she should get food for them so that they will not be mad. [S-T: PARTIALLY CORRECT]	
T: Any other ideas? Can anyone else think of a plan for Poppy? Student 4? [T-S: INVITE IDEAS]	
S4: I was the summarizer. [S-T: NR] First Poppy and Lungwort set out to ask Mr. Ocax for permission. Next, they found the tree and asked if they could move to the new house. Then, Mr. Ocax said no and they had to tell the family no. Lungwort was sad and went into his shoe. Poppy told her cousin she was going to find a new house on her own. [NEW ROLE]	

Note: Coding key:

T = Teacher   S = Student

Q = Question   T-S = Teacher-to-student interaction

S-T = Student-to-teacher interaction   NR = No response

S-S = Student-to-student interaction

Step 6: Analyze.

After three weeks, Kerri tape-recorded and transcribed a literature circle discussion and used this transcript and students' journals to understand how her students were participating in the literature circles and responding to the literature. A portion of this literature circle discussion of *Poppy* (Avi, 1995) is presented in Table 2.1. Kerri decided to do two things with the transcript: determine who was talking by counting the number of lines in the transcript where she or her students talked, and what they were talking about. Kerri noticed first and foremost that she was doing most of the work. Her contributions totaled thirty-four lines of the transcript, whereas the students carried twenty-five lines. Kerri also found that her students seemed anxious to get to their role in the literature circle. Despite her efforts to help students connect comments, students were simply waiting for their turn. When she asked a question to broaden thinking and called on students, they simply responded, "I was the [role]," and proceeded to talk about what they had prepared for the discussion. Kerri felt that the students' journals showed very surface responses without elaboration, such as "I like when Donovan was happy."

Step 7: Reflect.

Kerri knew she wanted students to discuss in the hopes of developing higher-level thinking about text, she knew she wanted them to respond, and she was providing a vehicle for discussion and modeling how to respond. Yet, it wasn't working. Kerri then reflected on the literature circle model itself. She felt that its structure might be preventing students from listening to one another and truly participating. They were so excited to share their own roles that they were not able to absorb what other students were saying. She also thought about their literature journals and realized that although she was modeling good responses, she did not provide anything concrete to help students determine what constituted a "good" response.

Kerri's reflection led her to cycle back to Step 3 (Ask) and rethink what she hoped to accomplish from her research.

Step 3: Ask.

Although Kerri's initial question was how to help her students make inferences about text, she realized there was more to it than that. She wanted her students to participate meaningfully in discussions and use writing as a way to think about literature. Kerri decided to simplify things for herself and her students. She chose to focus on one role presented in literature circles—the questioner. She felt that if she could help students ask meaningful questions about what they read, they might be more involved in reading and subsequent discussion. Here are her revised questions.

Teacher-as-Learner Questions
How can I teach my students to ask thoughtful questions and
participate meaningfully in group discussions? What can I do to
improve my students' response to literature?

Student-Learning Question
How will my students participate in group discussions
and respond to literature?

These different questions or goals required her to think differently about what she was doing.

Step 4: Plan.

Kerri planned to model how to ask thoughtful questions, record them on Post-it® notes, and place them on a specific part of the text. However, she realized that she also needed some scaffolds to help students generate thoughtful questions. She planned to provide students with question stems to assist them in differentiating what a "good" question might be. She used stems such as, "I wonder . . .," "I can't really understand . . .," and "I'm not sure . . . ." She also decided to provide some helpful starters that would generate thinking about text for the journal responses, such as "I was surprised . . ." and "I think . . . ."

Table 2.2 Kerri's Second Transcript

Seven Children (an old fable)	Analysis
T: You have just read *Seven Children*. What questions do you have about the fable? [T-S: INVITE QUESTIONS]	Amount of teacher talk: 8 lines
S1: I wondered why no one has names. [S-T: Q #1]	Amount of student talk: 26 lines
S2: I think the answer is because there were too many children. It would get confusing saying all those names. [S-S: CORRECT]	Mostly student-to-student interactions.
S1: Yes, but it gets confusing, like here in the story where it says [reads], " 'What should we do now,' said one of the seven children. 'I will decide since I am the oldest,' said the oldest. 'I am the smartest,' said the second oldest." Then it goes on and on and it gets confusing. [S-S: DISAGREE/SUPPORT]	Students answering each other's questions, responding to each other's comments.
S3: Yeah, because the smartest kid could have been at the end or something. [S-S: AGREE/SUPPORT]	Students providing support for answers.
S4: Yeah. It gets very confusing. I agree. [S-S: AGREE]	

(Continued)

Table 2.2 (Continued)

Seven Children (an old fable)	Analysis
S2: I guess I don't know why. [S-S: RESPOND TO DISAGREE]	Teacher serving to move discussion along, connect to text.
T: Do you think knowing their names was important to the plot of the story? Was it something you needed to know? [T-S: TEACHER PROBE]	Teacher's probes answered correctly.
S1, 2, & 3: No. [S-T: CORRECT]	Students turning over topic only after addressing comment or question that was on the table.
T: We can say it's an observation we have made about the story. Let's move on to another question. [T-S: EXPLAIN, REDIRECT]	
S4: Why are the kids so wild at the beginning of the story? [S-S: NEW Q #2]	
S5: They argue over what they wanted, almost like me and my sister do. [S-S: CORRECT, CONNECT]	
S1: They probably are close in age and have a problem getting along. [S-S: AGREE/SUPPORT]	
T: What have they not learned to do yet? [T-S: TEXT CONNECT]	
S7: They did not learn to work in unity. [S-T: CORRECT]	
S2: Well they have not learned to use teamwork yet. [S-S: REPHRASE]	
S3: Why did their father leave them alone in the woods? [S-S: NEW Q #3]	
S6: Because he wanted them to learn how to work as a team and use sportsmanship. So the mother gave them bundles to help them find their way home. [S-S: CORRECT]	
S2: Yeah, I agree, because the father and mother wanted them to learn they need to work together. The father had to leave right away. [S-S: AGREE/EXPAND]	
S4: I agree, too, because they needed the map that one child had and the food the other child had. [S-S: AGREE/SUPPORT]	
S5: And it would make them get along. [S-S: AGREE/SUPPORT]	
T: We have made some good points. [T-S: REINFORCE/RECAP]	

Step 5: Implement.

Kerri modeled stopping in text, posing a question using the question stems, and jotting the question on a Post-it note placed at the part of the text that prompted the question. She taught students how to participate in a group discussion using their Post-it questions. She explained and modeled how to respond to other classmates, how to provide evidence from the text to support what they were saying, and how to agree or disagree while providing evidence. She and the students created a checklist for a successful discussion. They practiced asking their questions, listening, and responding to each other. Kerri continued to model journal responses, but now used the various starters to show students how they could help them write a good response. She and the students then created a rubric for a good journal response. Kerri continued to collect the same data she had planned to collect—tape-recorded and transcribed discussions and journal responses.

Table 2.3 Kerri's Third Transcript

Holes, by Louis Sachar	Analysis
T: Who would like to start our discussion today? [T-S: INVITE DISCUSSION]	Amount of teacher talk: 9 lines
S1: In the chapter, X-Ray was acting weird because he kept switching his character. He was like starting to be mean to Stanley when he said, "What are you talking about?" Then at the end he was like saying Stanley was cool and the best. [S-S: CHARACTER OBSERVE #1/SUPPORT]	Amount of student talk: 34 lines Students listening to each other's questions, answering questions with support from text. Agreeing/ disagreeing with support. Teacher facilitating, inviting ideas, asking for support, and encouraging inferences. More teacher interaction, but functioning to spur deeper thinking.
T: Are there any other thoughts about this character's change in the chapters? [T-S: INVITE IDEAS]	
S2: I agree with what Student 1 was talking about X-Ray changing. In the beginning, X-Ray would not talk about the tube Stanley gave him. Maybe it's because Armpit said Warden had hidden cameras. That's why X-Ray would not talk about it with Stanley at that time. [S-T: AGREE/PROVIDE SUPPORT]	
S3: I have a question. When they are digging, why can't they just dump the dirt? [S-S: NEW Q#1]	
S4: They dump the dirt into previously dug holes because they do not want to dump it into their own holes because they are trying to see if they can find something else over there. [S-S: CORRECT] And I noticed that the warden is very bossy and mean. I wanted to know why they mention that her nails are painted bright red. [S-S: NEW OBSERVE CHARACTER #2]	

(Continued)

Table 2.3 (Continued)

Holes, by Louis Sachar	Analysis
T: Okay. So we are saying we have noticed something about a character in the story. [T-S: RECAP] You said she was bossy and mean. Who can tell me what told us that in the story? [T-S: TURN BACK]	
S4: You can tell the warden is bossy and mean because when X-Ray supposedly found something in the hole. She was telling Mr. Pendansky, "Fill the water bottles," and he said, "I just filled them two minutes ago." She said, "What did you say?" And then she told him again, "Fill the water bottles." She was being really argumentative with Mr. Pendansky. [S-T: CORRECT]	
S5: What is the warden's name? [S-S: NEW Q #2]	
T: Has the author told us what her name is? [T-S: PROBE]	
S1: The author has not said yet. They have just been calling her The Warden. [S-T: CORRECT]	
T: Why do we think she is acting the way she is? What is causing her to behave the way she is? [T-S: CONNECT/INFER]	
S1: Because she wants to find anything else that is with the gold tube. I think something is underground and she wants to know what it is. [S-T: CORRECT]	
S5: I agree with Student 1. I think she is looking for other things in the hole, too. [S-S: AGREE/RATIONALE]	
S6: I think she might be looking for something that belonged to Madame Zeroni. [S-S: AGREE/RATIONALE]	
S5: I disagree with Student 6 because Madame Zeroni never came to America so her things would not have ended up in Texas at Camp Green Lake. [S-S: DISAGREE/SUPPORT]	
S6: Yeah, that could be true. [S-S: AGREE]	

Step 6: Analyze.

After four weeks of additional instruction, Kerri tape-recorded and transcribed another discussion and began to analyze journal responses (see Table 2.2). She noted that students were participating in the discussion using the questions they had prepared. She also noticed her role was changing. She talked less, carrying eight lines of the transcript, whereas students carried twenty-six. In addition, her talk was focused on helping students connect to each other, rather than keeping herself as the center of

Figure 2.1 Kerri's Discussions. This chart shows the amount (percentage) of teacher and student talk during her three discussions. Kerri's talk decreased, while students' talk increased.

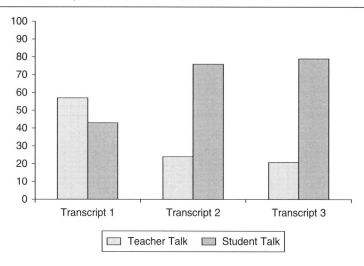

Table 2.4 Kerri's Students' Journal Entries

First Set of Journals	
I like when Donovan was happy.	Brief response, unelaborated; insufficient to assess text understanding (rubric = 0)
My favorite picture in the book is the one on page 65. I like it because it shows them being amazed with just words on pieces of paper.	Brief response, unelaborated; shows minimal understanding of text (rubric = 1)
I like the pitcher on page 53 because it is bright and colerful it also takes up the hole page.	Insufficient to assess text understanding (rubric = 0)
Second Set of Journals	
I wonder why he keeps taking about his grandfather. I know he was bad luck but he already said that. I also think there is going to be a yellow spotted lizzard coming around because Mr. Sur is trying to stop smoking he eats sunflowere seeds and the yellow spoted lizards eat sunflower seeds. If a yellow spotted lizzard comes I would run. That is what I think about these chapters.	Brief, relevant summary or reaction; few explanations followed by some evidence from the story; a fair understanding of the text (Rubric = 2)
I wonder why Stanley's dirty rotten pig stealing, not good great granpa stole Madden Zeronis pig? Shouldn't he know that she will cast a spell on him and his great great grandson? He should steal from other people's pig.	Brief, relevant summary or reaction; few explanations followed by some evidence from the story; a fair understanding of the text (Rubric = 2)

(Continued)

Table 2.4 (Continued)

Third Set of Journals	
I wonder why the Warden has been so nice to Stanley and mean to everybody else. Maybe because she some how knows that Stanley has found everything, not X-Ray. One part that she was nice to him is when she said "your doing fine. Just fine." I think there is some magic involved in the Warden!	Questions raised and answered; ideas are elaborated and adequate evidence from text is used to support ideas; good understanding of text (Rubric = 3)
I noticed that the Warden is very bossy! Maybe its because she wants to find what she wants to find. But what does she want to find? Maybe it has something to do with this mysterious KB person. I really like this book so far!	Questions raised and answered; ideas are elaborated and adequate evidence from text is used to support ideas; good understanding of text (Rubric = 3)

Figure 2.2 Kerri's Rubric Data. This chart shows the number of students that received each rubric score across the three times Kerri rated the responses against the rubric. Students moved from predominantly unelaborated responses to more developed and elaborated responses.

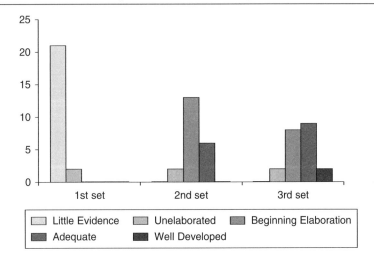

the group. Kerri found that students' journal responses were also improving, as measured by the rubric they had created. They moved from a 0–1 to a 2 (on a 0–4 scale). Students' responses included asking questions, elaborating on their responses, and connecting to other parts of text.

Step 7: Reflect.

Kerri's project was now going in the direction she wanted—students were purposeful, organized, and responding well. Kerri could see that her hard work was paying off. She chose to maintain her instruction as it was going. However, she made plans to continue to release more and more responsibility to the students, so they would become independent.

Step 6. Analyze.

After five more weeks, Kerri once again tape-recorded and transcribed the students' discussion and gathered their journals for analysis (see Table 2.3). She found the discussion was peer-led. Her role had decreased substantially (she spoke for nine lines, students for thirty-four). When she did contribute, it was to facilitate (connect or summarize) rather than lead. (You can see who talked across Kerri's three data points in Figure 2.1.) Students' journals also continued to improve, moving to a score of 3–4 on the rubric and showing good understanding of the text, questions, and interpretations based on evidence from the text. Excerpts from her students' journal entries across her project and a graph showing their progress are presented in Table 2.4 and Figure 2.2.

Stephanie's and Kerri's projects provide wonderful examples of the cyclical process of classroom research. They both began the process linearly, moving from the beginning step of noticing through implementing what they thought would work, and analyzing and reflecting on their data. From there, their process changed.

WRAP UP

The teacher vignettes in this chapter have captured the cyclical classroom research process as it unfolds. These teachers demonstrated reflection-on-action by stepping back and viewing what they had done so far and reflecting-in-action by adjusting as they went along. These are the parallels of reflection and research.

YOU TRY IT

Your task in Chapter 1 was to identify an area of need in your classroom. Now that you have narrowed your focus to a specific area, you are going to do two things:

- Investigate the research and practice in your area. Begin with a general question and move down the inquiry staircase shown in Figure 1.2.
- Once you have some guiding principles from the literature in place, narrow down your inquiry to a specific question you would like to answer through research.

3

Dealing With Data

Data is critical to understanding the teaching and learning issues you face in the classroom. In this chapter we will explore ways of analyzing the different kinds of data you have collected for different kinds of questions.

ANALYZING PRODUCT-FOCUSED (NUMERICAL) DATA

Some people find numbers intimidating. However, in practice, making sense out of product-focused (*numerical* or *quantitative*) data is fairly straight-forward. A simple chart or graph can help you "see" students' assessment scores or progress at various points along the way. Here are some general questions to guide your thinking about how to analyze numbers.

Question 1: Compared to What?

Let us look at some of the data that teachers face every day and think about what these data tell us. If a tenth-grade student takes a standard-ized, group-administered reading assessment and earns a reading com-prehension score of 475, is that good? If a second grader receives an 80 on a classroom spelling test, is that good? How about if a sixth grader receives 25 points on a literature response assignment, is that good? The answer to all of these questions is, "It depends." It depends on what is expected. Numerical data must have a reference for you to make sense of it. The first question you need to ask when looking at numerical data is, "Compared to what?" Let us use these hypothetical reading comprehension, spelling, and literature response assignment scores as examples.

The reading comprehension is a standardized test, also called a norm-referenced test. The publishers of standardized tests provide you with the information you need to understand how your scores compare to a reference group, or norm. (You will find examples of norm-referenced literacy assessments in Table 3.1.) If you know the mean (the "average" or 50th percentile) score for the test and its standard deviation (the average amount of wiggle room acceptable across the scores), then you can determine whether your student's score of 475 is "good." Let us say that the mean (the average) for the test is 500 and the standard deviation is 50. This means the average range is 450–550. Now that you know the reference point, you can understand where your student's score fits in the scheme of this reading comprehension test—the student is in the average range. Many standardized literacy assessments have a mean of 100 and a standard deviation of 15. However, since the means and standard deviations change depending upon the test, it is easier to look at your student's percentile score. Your tenth grader's reading comprehension score of 475 is in the 30th percentile, which means the student did as well or better than 30 percent of the tenth graders who took the test in the norming sample.

Table 3.1 Examples of Norm-Referenced Literacy Assessments

Assessment Title	Type	Publisher
Gates-MacGinitie Reading Test	Group	Riverside Publishing
Gray Oral Reading Test	Individual	Pearson
Group Reading Assessment and Diagnostic Evaluation	Group	Pearson Learning Group
Stanford Diagnostic Reading Test	Individual	Harcourt Assessment
Woodcock Reading Mastery Test— Revised/NU	Individual	Pearson
Woodcock-Johnson III Diagnostic Reading Battery	Individual	Riverside Publishing

Your second grader's 80 percent on a spelling test means that the student spelled 80 percent (eight out of ten, 16 out of 20, etc.) of the words correctly. However, to interpret this score, you need to know what 80 percent means with respect to expectations. In many schools, 80 percent is the equivalent of a B or B-, which most people would find respectable. However, perhaps your school has a criterion for complete mastery. In that case, students would be expected to spell 100 percent of the words correctly. This student's score of 80 percent would then be viewed as lower than expected.

The 25 points your sixth grader received on the literature response assignment needs to be viewed with respect to the total possible points the student could have received. Let us say that the assignment was worth 50 possible points. The student earned 50 percent, or half of the total points. Is that good? That depends. You need once again to know what the expectations are. If the score is based on a typical grading system (A, B, C, etc.), then the answer will be "no." The teacher probably expects students to earn at least a grade of B (80 percent of the possible points) or C (70 percent). In another case, however, earning 25 points might be good if the average number of points that students usually earn is 27. This student's score is average.

Question 2: Which Numbers Should I Use?

Once you determine the reference to interpret the numbers, you need to decide what numbers you want to compare. For example, do you want to compare each student's scores (Student 1's scores were 59 before you started and 85 at the end; Student 2's scores were 91 before and 93 after), or do you want to compare the group's scores (the average score for the class at the beginning was 75, at the end, 82). These comparisons can lead to different conclusions. For example, let us say I have ten students in my classroom and I am comparing their grades. The average grade for my students before I began my research was 60 percent, and at the end of the year it had risen to 85 percent. I can say that, on average, my students improved. However, did all students improve? Did all students improve equally? Looking at individual student data may show me that some students improved a great deal, but others showed no improvement at all. To see these comparisons visually, look at Figures 3.1, 3.2, and 3.3. Figure 3.1 shows the class's scores on average for the beginning and end of an intervention program. It is obvious that students made progress. However, it is not obvious who made what kind of progress. Figures 3.2 and 3.3 show different pictures of each student's progress from the beginning to the end of the intervention. Each of these three pictures is a valid way to present the data, but each helps us understand the data in a different way. To tell the story you want to tell, you need to think about how you should present the numbers.

Question 3: What Comparison Should I Make?

In addition to determining the reference and which numbers you wish to compare, you need to think about what comparisons you should make. We usually interpret standardized test results based on the reference sample. For example, given a reading test with a mean of 100 and a standard deviation of 15, we know that a student's score of 85 is a standard deviation ("significantly") below the mean. That is one piece of

Figure 3.1 This graph represents the average pre- and post-intervention scores of a group of ten students who took a standardized assessment with a mean of 100 and a standard deviation of 15. "At a glance" you can see that the group average rose by about 5 points. We cannot see whether each student improved, or to what extent.

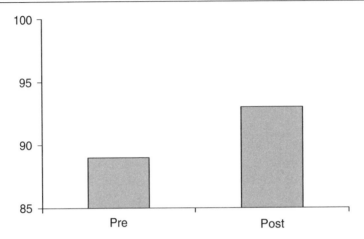

Figure 3.2 This graph represents each of the ten students' pre- and post-intervention scores on the same standardized measure as in Figure 3.1. A quick glance at this graph helps us see that every student except Olivia and Melissa made progress and that Jamie and Jay made the greatest gains.

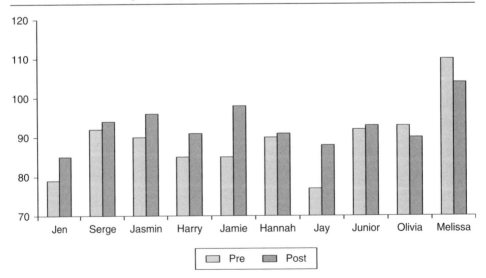

Figure 3.3 This graph represents the same data from the same ten students presented in Figures 3.1 and 3.2, and, like Figure 3.2, is a graph of progress. However, Figure 3.2, with double bars for each of ten students, seems cluttered. This graph, simply showing the amount of gain each of the ten students made (in Standard Score units) from beginning to end of the intervention, is the clearest indicator of progress. Right away, a teacher can see "at a glance" who needs additional help.

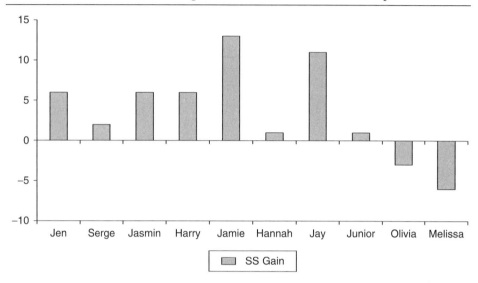

information, or one way to look at the score. Now let us say that you already knew that your student was a struggling reader. Finding out that the student is "below average" does nothing but confirm what you already knew. However, what if you compared the student's scores at different points in time, or in relation to the student's *own* scores, rather than comparing the student with the reference group of the test? For example, let us say that your student initially attained a standard score of 70 on the standardized reading test and then received intensive tutoring for one year. The student's score now is 85. Comparing this score to the mean of the test simply tells you that the student continues to struggle. However, comparing the student's ending and beginning scores gives you a different picture. This student gained 15 standard score points, one full standard deviation. That is a lot of progress! Yes, the student is still "behind," but looking within the student's scores shows progress.

Question 4: How Do I Decide What Numbers and What Comparison?

To decide what numbers to use and how to use them, first go back to your original research question. What did you want to know? Second, look at your data. What does it look like? Let us say that a teacher has been working with fourth-grade students to improve their spelling. The teacher has their beginning of the year scores on a developmental spelling inventory and has given another assessment midway through the year. The teacher averages the students' spelling scores for both of these data points (see Figure 3.4) and finds that students have made some, but not a lot of progress. However, looking at the actual assessments, the teacher notices that students who struggled the most initially seemed to make more progress than the average data indicates. Conversely, students who were already good spellers seemed to make little progress. There is a good reason for this. The above average students were already spelling above what would be expected for their grade. So, although they appeared to make no progress, they did not have much room to grow. Looking at the class average was not a good idea. To tell the story that students' gains in spelling seemed dependent upon their beginning skills, this teacher could look at the data based on students' initial spelling ability (weak spellers, average spellers, and above-average spellers). Grouping the students' data first, then averaging their progress by group shows a different picture (see Figure 3.5).

Figure 3.4 Average Scores for a Fourth-Grade Classroom on a Developmental Spelling Task Where the Highest Possible Score Is 62

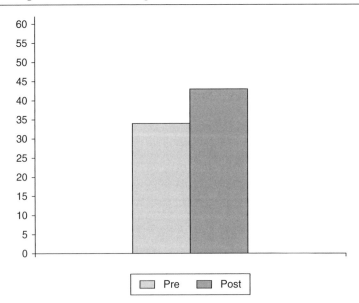

Figure 3.5 Average Gain in Spelling Feature Points for Students Represented in Figure 3.4, Based on Their Initial Spelling Ability

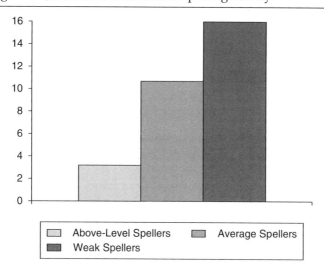

Above-Level Spellers   Average Spellers
Weak Spellers

ANALYZING PROCESS-FOCUSED DATA

Process data, such as notes, transcripts of lessons, and interviews, are information-rich, yet complicated to analyze. In order to truly understand these data, you need to get to know them well through reading, rereading, and rereading them again.

Coding Data: Open Coding.

The most common way that researchers go about making sense out of process data is by coding it into salient themes. Since word sorting is one literacy practice featured in this book, I will use that as an analogy for the process of coding data (see Figure 3.6).

Let us say we are conducting an open word sort—sorting words into categories without knowing beforehand what categories are represented. We would most likely start to notice some features of the words and group them accordingly. Then we would check our groups to see if the words in each group made sense given what we were thinking. We may realize that some of the words do not fit the pattern and need to be moved. We keep at this until we are sure that we have sorted our words in a way that makes sense and follows a pattern. Then we try to come to some conclusions about what that pattern is telling us.

The same is true for process-focused data. You read through your data and make notes about the salient points or themes you see. Then you will

Figure 3.6 Open Word Sorting as an Analogy for Coding Process-Focused Data

Here are my word cards:

First round of analysis:

- Hypothesize: The words all begin with the /k/ sound.
- Sort: No need to sort. All belong in the same category.
- Review: Yes, they all begin with the /k/ sound.

Second round of analysis:

- Re-examine: Is there any difference between the words?
- Hypothesize: Some words begin with "c" and some with "k."
- Sort:

- Review: Yes, these words begin either with "c" or "k."

Third round of analysis:
- Re-examine: Is there anything else uniform about the words in each column?
- Hypothesize: I might be able to group them by the vowel that comes after the "c" or "k."
- Sort:

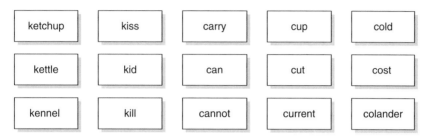

ketchup	kiss	carry	cup	cold
kettle	kid	can	cut	cost
kennel	kill	cannot	current	colander

- Review: Yes, I can group them this way.

Fourth round of analysis:
- Re-examine: Is there any other way I can divide these up?
- Hypothesize: No, I am satisfied that each category represents something distinct.

Question: What is this data trying to tell me?

Interpretation: I think this is trying to tell me that there are two ways to spell the sound of /k/–with a "c" or with a "k." I should use a "c" before a, u, or o; I should use a "k" before e or i.

---

read your initial notes to determine whether any of the notes go together. You will begin to categorize your data and continue this process until you are sure that each item you have in each category represents the same idea. Making a copy of the data is helpful—you can cut up the data and paste pieces onto index cards or otherwise move and sort, write on, or color-code them. Once you are satisfied that each piece of data in each category represents that category, you will need to decide what each category is all about.

Step 1

Let us use the interview data in Table 3.2 as an example of open coding. In these interviews, the teachers were answering a very general prompt: "Discuss central issues in your teaching." In an initial read through this data, look for and underline words that the teachers used again and again. The first word you probably noted being repeated is *believe*. You would underline each time *believe* appears, and review to make sure all are underlined. In these data, there are also words that, in the context of what the teachers are saying, are synonymous with *believe*: *feel* and

Table 3.2 Coded Excerpts From Two Teacher Interviews, Where Teachers Were Asked to Discuss Central Issues in Their Teaching

TEACHER 1

I am such a person that <u>believes</u> that *everybody can do things. You can always better yourself* no matter what. **Everybody can meet a <u>goal</u>, it might take you ten steps to meet a <u>goal</u>** when **another kid it takes two steps but we all can do it.** You just need to *push and work* for it and *strive to do it.* So that's how I am. I have always <u>believed</u> that way and I have kids and *they'll do whatever the <u>goal</u> is and they succeed on it.* I will move them on to something different but the rest of the kids who still haven't gotten it, I will *sit with you and we will get it* and we will *work on it.* So I am a true <u>believer</u> of that, *I don't care how long it takes you to get it,* we will *work on it* together and I will keep moving these kids on and have them **learn at their level,** but you need to *keep working.* When I have **kids that just refuse** and **parents that don't help** them that **goes against what my <u>belief</u> is,** no *that kid can learn that.* I understand that they **aren't able to do it right away** but they can if they *work on it.* When I have *someone say no forget about it* they aren't going to do it, he isn't going to learn that, he doesn't want to learn, he hates reading; when I get that it just *goes against my beliefs,* so that *makes it difficult.* Sometimes you can get through that and the kids can get pushed but sometimes *it is so hard to get through it.* My push is that *everyone can do it* and you just *stick with it.* It **might take me a long time** and staying after school and working with them, **but I do it.**

Step 1: Underline words repeated across the transcript:

- <u>Beliefs</u>
- <u>Goals</u>

Step 2: Code what the person says about each repeated word:

<u>Beliefs</u> (italicized):

- Everyone can succeed
- Work to meet goals
- Keep working/striving and you will meet goals
- Things go against beliefs

<u>Goals</u> (bolded):

- Set goals
- Everyone can meet goals
- Work where kids are so they can achieve goals
- Time doesn't matter, reaching goals matters

Step 3. Explain "going against beliefs" (bold italic):

People can go against what she believes:

- Parents
- People who don't believe
- Kids

Things that go against make teaching hard

know. You would underline these as well. Jot in the margins of both transcripts: *beliefs.*

Step 2

Next, read through the transcripts again to determine what teachers were saying about *beliefs.* Bold the contexts where they discuss *beliefs.* You would then repeat Steps 1 and 2 with other words you found recurring until you had outlined and defined each.

(Continued)

TEACHER 2	**Step 1: Underline words repeated across the transcript:**
I feel very <u>conflicted</u> right now because what I <u>believe</u> that these **children really need to help them** is, <u>I can't do</u> that for them because there's **too many of them** and because I also have to teach, not only is there the literacy piece, but there's the math piece, and there's science and there's social studies. Now all of a sudden we've got these science tests coming up. They're now testing on science as well. We *hardly have any time to teach* science and social studies as it is. So I guess what I really <u>feel</u> would **help these children** <u>isn't what I can do</u>. So I go in there every day and I teach, and I know that sometimes what I'm doing is **not beneficial for everybody**. It's probably going to be okay for the students that are functioning above level or be alright with those average kids, but those ones that are below level, sometimes they're lost. But I have to go with what I have. To give a child an instructional program **on their level** that's **what they really need** is a **lot of work**. And it's not that I walk out the door at 2:50 everyday, because I certainly don't. But with the **amount of things that are required** by teachers, the **amount of paperwork** in terms of the PLPs and giving the DIBELS assessment, *there's not a lot of <u>time</u>*. To plan instructional reading groups, right now I have **one, two, three, four instructional reading groups**. That takes *<u>hours and hours</u> to really plan* that kind of a lesson and then you turn around and I **still have to plan five days worth of math lessons**. I try to pick problems for different . . . for the kids' **instructional level** in math, too. So *it's a <u>time</u> thing*. What I <u>know</u> would **work best for these kids,** a lot of times <u>I can't do it</u> because there's *just no time*.	• <u>Beliefs</u> • <u>Can't do</u> • <u>Time</u> **Step 2: Code what the person says about each repeated word:** <u>Beliefs:</u> • Kids need help • Need instruction on level <u>Can't do</u> (Against Beliefs): • Too many students • Too much work • Too many requirements/ mandates <u>Time:</u> • No time to teach • No time to plan

Step 3

Once you have coded the data, you need to make sense out of it—to pull it together in some cogent way. This means taking the codes from Steps 1 and 2 and grouping them again. In these data, you could collapse the codes into two main categories: *what I believe, what goes against what I believe*. For these two teachers then, when asked to discuss *central* issues in their teaching, they both chose to talk about beliefs and challenges to those beliefs. Their beliefs and challenges showed commonalities—meeting students where they are, issues of time, and workload, but within these their focus was different. For example, Teacher 1 discussed time—it takes a lot of time to help students succeed, but despite this, she will take the time to help students succeed; Teacher 2 focuses on time—it takes too much time to plan and meet school requirements and mandates, so she does not have the time to do it all.

Coding Data: Closed Coding.

Another way to code qualitative data is to begin with specific questions or foci. To follow the word sorting analogy, this is like a closed sort. For example, if I had videotaped the writing classes I discussed in Chapter 1 to understand how students talk about writing, I may have analyzed the data with that specific question in mind. How do students provide feedback for revision? Do they tell each other what to do? Do they ask questions? I could then first separate my data by telling comments versus asking comments. Then within those, I could begin to code for patterns.

Coding Data: Pre-Existing Codes.

Yet another way to analyze qualitative data is through a pre-existing coding system. For example, a colleague of mine is looking at the kinds of questions preservice teachers ask when they are teaching science. She decided to use Bloom's taxonomy (Bloom, 1984) as a frame for coding the questions. She will first go through the transcripts and identify questions. She will then code each question based on the descriptions presented in each level of the taxonomy. Once she does this, she may decide she needs to go further (for example, are there times when teachers are more likely to ask a particular kind of question), but she at least has a way to talk about the questions teachers ask.

WRAP UP

There are many types of data you can collect. There are also many ways to analyze data. In this chapter you have seen that your data collection and analysis both need to target the question you are asking. When analyzing data, first think about what you want to know, then choose a method of analysis that will help you answer your question. People are sometimes skeptical of numerical data, feeling as though a researcher can manipulate it to a certain end. That is not really true, but researchers can choose to present data in different ways. If you choose to show the average of your class as a whole, you miss individual data; if you choose to show individual data, you might not be able to quickly show someone else, perhaps a school administrator, how your class did as a whole. Choose wisely how you present your numbers to ensure you are making the best comparisons to explain your data.

YOU TRY IT

To help you deal with data, you will step outside the inquiry you began with the tasks from Chapters 1 and 2 to practice coding data.

- Using the transcripts in Table 3.2 and this chapter's discussion about coding these transcripts, try to code other segments of these two teacher's interviews provided in Appendix A. Here, the teachers are talking about their role in assessment and how assessment informs their instruction.

Part II

Teachers' Classroom Research in Literacy

Now that we have explored the classroom research process, we will examine how this plays out in literacy teaching and learning. In this part of the book, teachers share their research projects. These projects focus on exploring teaching practices and negotiating school and district expectations (Section 1), as well as translating research to practice (Section 2). Because these chapters are actual teacher research projects, they focus on particular age groups or grades of students. However, each project can easily be adapted to any appropriate grade. At the end of each chapter, in addition to the *Wrap Up* and *You Try It* sections, a section titled *How Does This Project Relate to You?* provides ideas for exploring the same topic with your students.

Each chapter in this part of the book provides an example of the cycle of classroom research. Therefore, you need not read these chapters in order but should feel free to investigate whatever topics appeal to you most strongly. To help you negotiate Part II, I have included "spotlights" within each chapter. One spotlight highlights an aspect of classroom research that is particularly well represented in the chapter. The other spotlights represent literacy topics and teacher practices. Each of the literacy topics focuses on one of the five core areas of literacy (phonemic awareness, phonics, fluency, vocabulary, and comprehension).

Here is a preview of the classroom research and literacy spotlights.

Chapter	Classroom Research Spotlights	Literacy Spotlights
4	Step 6: Analyzing data Coding process-focused data	Teacher: Discussion Students: Comprehension
5	Step 5: Implement Logistics for organizing data	Teacher: Choosing and using literacy assessments Students: Early literacy
6	Step 4: Plan	Teacher: Differentiating literacy instruction Students: Word study
7	Step 2: Inquire Step 8: Plan	Vocabulary teaching and learning
8	Step 6: Analyze Step 7: Reflect	Fluency
9	Steps 3–8: Cycling through the process	Phonics and phonemic awareness
10	Step 1: Notice Step 3: Ask	Vocabulary (morphology)

Looking at Teaching Within Mandated Programs

In the age of accountability, mandates pose a particular challenge to teachers in general and to classroom research. Teachers may want to try something new in a careful, systematic way but are not able to do so because their district requires them to use a specific program. The three teachers you will meet in this section conducted their research in schools that, if not mandated, at least *strongly suggested* that they use a particular program or administer a particular assessment. Each found a way to continue to do what was mandated, yet explore something new at the same time. One of the benefits of classroom research is that you can use carefully gathered and analyzed data to show other stakeholders that one method does not necessarily meet everyone's needs. These teachers were able to use their classroom research to broach the subject of mandates and show administrators that other methods are successful—maybe more so that the current model.

Reading Aloud

Do I Really *Sound Like That?*

Classroom Research Spotlight
Step 6: Analyzing Data

Literacy Spotlight
Teacher: Discussion practices
Students: Comprehension

Good teaching is a big factor in student achievement. But how do we look at our teaching? One way to take a critical look at our practice is to have someone else look at it for us. An objective observer can tell us a lot about what we are doing. But that is not always possible or practical. Classroom research provides a great opportunity to focus on *seeing* our teaching.

In this chapter, Maureen, a K–1 multi-age teacher, uses audiotaping and transcript analysis to understand her read-aloud and discussion practices. Because Maureen was on maternity leave, her project was short-lived. She followed the eight steps but did not recursively cycle through planning, implementing, analyzing, and reflecting. However, her question really required her to look deeply and critically at her current practice. Two sessions of reading aloud provided enough data for her to examine. Her project is included here because it showcases how to look at your own practice, even if you are not currently in a position to change it. Maureen's project represents the idea of *reflection-on-action*—looking back to reflect on our teaching and thinking about what this means for future teaching. This leads to the first tip for classroom research.

Classroom Research Tip #1:
It's possible to conduct classroom research
even when you're not in the classroom.

MAUREEN'S RESEARCH

Context for Maureen's Project.

Maureen teaches a multi-age combined kindergarten and first-grade classroom within a K–4 elementary school in a small, suburban school district. The student population is predominantly White of moderate income. Many children from nearby naval housing attend her school, which increases student mobility. (The school's mobility index is 45 percent.) The school is classified as "moderately performing."

Maureen's school uses a basal reading series as its primary means of literacy instruction. What Maureen learned about how discussion practices support comprehension did not necessarily coincide with what the basal reader suggested. In addition to presenting her research, this chapter also represents one way to show the difference between two methods of instruction.

Step 1: Maureen Observes Her Students and Her Practice.

Maureen had been learning about read-aloud strategies during a graduate course she was taking. She reflected on what she was learning: "Since I teach a multi-age K–1 group of students, many of my students are not yet reading texts. Read aloud really is an important part of my instruction. It's not just fun time. It's a time when I can focus on comprehension. We had been talking about read aloud in one of my graduate courses and I began thinking how different my read aloud seemed from what I was learning about, and wondered whether my students were getting the most out of it this time."

Step 2: Maureen Inquires Into Her Focus Area.

Maureen learned a lot about reading aloud to children. The first point, that reading aloud is important, she already knew in her heart. What she was not aware of was the research that really looked into read aloud and described what was going on and what should be going on. Here are the ideas Maureen found most useful.

Read Aloud Is Important

Reading aloud to young children is a practice that is well documented by research. In the landmark report *Becoming a Nation of Readers*, the Commission on Reading stated, "The single most important activity for building the knowledge and skills required for eventual success in reading is reading aloud to children" (Anderson, Hiebert, Scott, & Wilkinson, 1985,

p. 23). By reading aloud, the teacher exposes students to a variety of texts and models fluent, expressive reading so that students know what reading should sound like. The teacher helps students understand concepts of print (Clay, 1991), print functions (what print is for) (Purcell-Gates, 1998), and story structure (Morrow, 1985), as well as gain comprehension (Morrow, 1990), vocabulary, and language development (Feitelson, Goldstein, Eshel, Flasher, Levin, & Sharon, 1991). Perhaps the most valuable benefit of reading aloud is that it gives children experience with *decontextualized language*—the language of books. Students need to understand that book language is not the same as talking language and that book events do not happen in real time (Snow & Ninio, 1986). Calkins (2000) discusses that in order to talk about a read aloud, children must first listen and build the world of the story in their minds.

The Way Teachers Structure the Read-Aloud Activity Makes a Difference

There are different ways teachers read aloud. Some teachers read a book cover-to-cover without stopping to discuss the text. Others discuss the text before and after reading, while others stop throughout the text to talk about the story. Each type of read-aloud practice has its own benefits. However, "co-construction" reading, read-aloud that includes teachers and students engaging in a large amount of analytic talk (predicting, explaining vocabulary, analyzing characters, etc.) *during* reading, is strongly related to vocabulary and story structure skills (Dickinson & Smith, 1994).

Comprehension Is Active

Co-construction—actively engaging children with the text ideas—is based on an understanding that comprehension is a constructive process and requires readers and listeners to be *active* (Beck & McKeown, 2001). Students need to work at understanding; they cannot sit passively and "get" the ideas in a text.

Teachers do not always practice co-construction read aloud. In many kindergarten and first-grade classrooms, teachers ask questions that require students to merely retrieve facts from the text, which actually reduces, rather than enhances, the quality of students' responses (Beck & McKeown, 2001). Because teachers ask retrieval questions, the responses students give may not accurately reflect their understanding of the text (Beck & McKeown, 2001; Goldenberg, 1993). For example, a student might be able to retrieve a fact from the text but not understand how that fact relates to others in the text or how to draw inferences from it.

Important Ideas in Reading Aloud

Prior planning is absolutely essential (Beck & McKeown, 2001; Beck, McKeown, Hamilton, & Kucan, 1997; Goldenberg, 1993). Before reading aloud, the teacher must identify the big issues of the story and anticipate where students might misunderstand. This helps the teacher decide where in the text to stop and discuss and develop queries that relate to the most important concepts.

Text Talk (Beck & McKeown, 2001) is one model of read-aloud that helps teachers scaffold students' understanding. In *Text Talk*, the teacher asks open-ended questions, *queries*, that require students to reflect on story ideas rather than simply retrieve facts. Teachers also conduct only a brief pre-reading discussion, just enough to activate prior knowledge, and show pictures judiciously, sometimes waiting until they have discussed that segment of text. This is because young children can over-rely on background knowledge and often construct meaning by looking at the pictures, rather than listening to the story (Beck & McKeown, 2001).

Step 3: Maureen Develops Specific Questions.

Maureen was interested in learning two things for and about herself, so she had two teacher-as-learner questions. However, in order to understand herself, she needed to look at how students responded to her practice as well. Maureen wrote, "I use the Houghton Mifflin basal series in my classroom. I read aloud many stories because they are at a higher level than my students can read themselves. The basal teacher's guide gives questions the teacher should ask the students. When thinking about what I read about reading aloud, and the *Text Talk* model, I began wondering whether there would be a difference between my discussions with my students using the basal versus if I planned according to *Text Talk*." Here are Maureen's questions.

Teacher-as-Learner Questions
How do I create and implement a *Text Talk* plan?
If I created and used *Text Talks*, would my discussions be different than when I base my read-aloud on the basal reader's suggested questions?

Student Learning Question
Would implementing a *Text Talk* discussion encourage students to respond more critically and improve the quality of their thinking?

Step 4: Maureen Formulates a Plan.
Planning Logistics

Maureen had unusual logistics to overcome—she was not actually teaching at the time she conducted this research. However, she did not want to wait until her return to the classroom to look at her practice. Maureen wrote, "The first thing I needed to do was to figure out where I was going to do this research. I was on maternity leave, but wanted to be ready to begin a new kind of read aloud when I returned if I found that *Text Talk* seemed to be a better model. Rather than go back to my own classroom (I didn't think that would be good for the substitute!), I asked a colleague if I could read aloud in her second-grade classroom. Since I was really focused on taking a look at a specific part of my practice, rather than whether students gained a particular skill, this seemed OK."

Planning Instruction

The first step in preparing a good *Text Talk* is choosing the right book. Beck and McKeown (2001) give several criteria for choosing a picture storybook to read aloud.

- The story should be harder than students can read on their own, but not so hard that they can't understand it if read aloud.
- The story should follow traditional story structure (characters, setting, problem, events, resolution, theme).
- The story should be told primarily through the words, rather than the pictures.

Maureen needed to choose two texts to compare the two models of read aloud. She also needed stories that the teacher had not yet read to or with her second-grade students. Maureen chose *Ruby the Copycat* (Rathman, 1991) from the second-grade basal reader. Next Maureen needed an appropriate story for her *Text Talk*. This was a little tricky because she was concerned about how much the story itself might have to do with how the discussion unfolded. She wrote, "I wanted to make sure that I was able to see the difference in the two discussion types, rather than any difference in how students might respond to the stories themselves. I realize this is hard to do, since students like some stories more than others, but I thought if I selected stories by the same author that shared a similar theme, it might help eliminate some of the story effects."

Maureen chose *Officer Buckle and Gloria* (Rathman, 1995) as her *Text Talk* book. It is also read commonly in second grade and was recommended by the teacher; the teacher had not yet read it to her students.

Planning the Discussions

Planning the basal discussion was straightforward. Maureen simply needed to follow the suggestions in the teacher's manual. To make it easier to follow these suggestions when she was reading aloud, she wrote the basal questions on Post-it notes and placed them directly within the book itself.

Planning for the *Text Talk* was a little harder. Beck and McKeown (2001) suggest these steps:

- Read the story and summarize it. (Create a story map if needed.)
- Identify the "big issues" or major ideas the students should understand.

- Identify ideas that might be confusing or that students might mis-understand.
- Taking the ideas students should understand and the possible points of confusion, decide where in the story to stop and discuss the text.
- At each stopping point, develop open-ended queries asking students to explain, analyze, etc.
- Write the queries on Post-it notes and secure to the appropriate place within the text.
- Think about how students might respond to each query. Be ready to help them dig deeper by preparing a follow-up query. Write the follow-up query on the Post-it note under the initial question.

Using these guidelines, Maureen created her *Text Talk* script for *Officer Buckle and Gloria* (see Appendix B). She also determined, in advance, which illustrations she would show before reading the text and which ones she would show after reading and discussing the text segment. She included these in her plan. Once again, Maureen wrote the queries, the responses she expected from students (what information they should understand), and follow-up queries on Post-it notes and placed them on the appropriate points within the story.

Planning Data Collection

To view her own practice Maureen needed to capture the discussions as they were happening. She decided to audiotape the discussions and transcribe them. To make transcribing easier, Maureen did some pre-transcribing work to get ready for her data.

- She typed the text of each story into separate documents.
- She typed into the appropriate places within each story the queries, expected responses, and follow-ups she had already pre-planned.

This way when she was ready to do the actual transcription, she had a lot of it already done. She then only needed to listen to her tapes, revise any queries to reflect what she actually asked, and type the students' comments and her follow-up responses.

Step 5: Maureen Implements Her Plan and Collects Data.

Logistics

Maureen was conducting the discussions in another teacher's classroom. She knew some of the students from having taught them in first grade; others she had never met. She wanted to make sure the students felt comfortable working with her before she actually conducted the first discussion. She made a date to meet the students and talk to them about her project. Because any kind of equipment is always a curiosity to young children, she explained that she would be tape-recording their discussions. She let the students practice talking into the tape recorder and listening to their voices.

Classroom Research Tip #2:
LOGISTICS
If you audio- or video-record your practice,
test out your recording equipment first!

Instruction

Maureen conducted the discussions on two consecutive weeks, first conducting the basal discussion, then the *Text Talk*. Each discussion lasted thirty to forty minutes. Prior to each discussion, Maureen reminded the students to project their voices when speaking so that the recorder would pick up their responses.

Maureen's implementation was short-lived and straightforward. Figuring out what it meant was more challenging.

Step 6: Maureen Analyzes the Data.

Coding the Transcripts

Probably the most difficult part of Maureen's research was analyzing her data. Even though she only conducted two discussions, she had a lot of data. She analyzed her data much like the examples in Chapter 3. The easiest way to describe how Maureen went about this process is to take it in steps.

Transcribe the Discussions

Because Maureen had pre-planned her transcription by typing in the text, questions, and follow-ups, she had a lot of work already done. She went back to her saved files, listened to her tapes, and added her and the students' comments.

Figure Out What to Do With Those Transcripts

Now that Maureen had accurate documentation of the discussions, she needed to determine how to approach thinking about what they meant. Maureen wrote, "The hardest thing for me was figuring out what to do with the transcripts. How was I going to compare them? I knew I needed to code the questions and student responses. I began by just reading the transcripts over and over again, to think about what I was asking students and how I was responding to them."

Separate Initial Queries, Follow-Up Queries, and Responses

Maureen decided to separately code her initial queries (the first query she asked students at each stopping point), follow-up queries (what she asked after students answered the initial query), and responses (what she said to students after they responded). Before she identified codes, she first went through the transcripts and highlighted initial queries, follow-up queries, and responses with different colored highlighters.

Develop a Coding System to Categorize the Queries and Responses

Maureen read through the transcripts and labeled each initial query according to what she was asking students to do. She kept track of these in a table to make sure she was giving the same label to the same type of queries. After coding the initial queries, Maureen began the same process with the follow-up queries, then the responses.

Recheck the Codes

When Maureen completed the initial coding, she went back to make sure that her coding made sense. At first, she coded lots of queries as "infer," meaning that she was asking students to read between the lines. However, looking at all of these inference queries, she noted that they seemed qualitatively different. Students could answer some by relying on personal experience. For example, to answer the question, "How do you think Ruby felt on the first day [of school]?", students could simply respond with how they felt on the first day. Students needed to connect text pieces to answer other inferential queries such as, "When Officer Buckle looks back, Gloria is sitting at attention. What does this tell us about Gloria?" This difference was important to Maureen, so she went back through and recoded all inference queries as either "personal inferences" or "text inferences." She continued going back and forth through her transcripts until she was satisfied that her labels adequately captured what was going on. Maureen's final codes for initial queries are in Table 4.1, follow-ups queries and responses are in Table 4.2.

Code Student Responses

After she coded her queries and responses, Maureen began coding the students' responses. To make it manageable, she decided to simply code whether the students answered the questions correctly, incorrectly, or incompletely (see Table 4.3).

Compare

Once she coded all data, she put them into an Excel spreadsheet and made charts to compare the frequency of each type of query and response between the two discussions (see Figures 4.1, 4.2, and 4.3).

Table 4.1 Maureen's Codes for Initial Questions and Queries

Code	Explanation	Example
Retrieve	Requires students to recall specific information explicitly stated in the text or illustrated in the picture	What do we know about Gloria? How did Ruby try to be like Angela?
Summarize	Asks students to summarize events but allows for interpretation	What's going on? What do we know so far?
Text Inference	Requires students to make a text- or picture-based inference; requires students to make a prediction (forward inference)	When Officer Buckle looks back, Gloria is sitting at attention. What does this tell us about Gloria?
Personal Inference or Connection	Requires students to make an inference that could be based solely on their own personal experience; requires students to connect the text to personal experience	How do you think Ruby feels on her first day? How would you feel on the first day of school?
Vocabulary	Requires students to explain vocabulary, a literary phrase, or mstory title	So what does it mean, "the audience roared"?
Evaluate	Requires students to express an opinion	What do you think about the way Angela acted?
Compare	Requires students to compare and contrast	Compare and contrast Angela's feelings from Monday to Friday.

Table 4.2 Maureen's Codes for Follow-Up Queries and Responses

Follow-Up Codes	Explanation	Example
QUERIES		
Narrow	Teacher helps students make an inference not yet achieved by asking them to retrieve smaller pieces of text or define vocabulary	What are they really laughing at? Does he realize what Gloria is doing?
	Teacher rereads portion of text to narrow information students need to make inference	[Re-Reading] *When Officer Buckle looks back, Gloria is sitting at attention.* What does this tell us about Gloria?
Explain	Teacher asks students to explain or support answers by providing evidence	Why? What makes you think that?

(Continued)

Table 4.2 (Continued)

Follow-Up Codes	Explanation	Example
QUERIES		
Repeat	Teacher asks student to answer a question already answered by another student	Teacher: What do you think about the way Angela acted? Kristen? K: Very mean Teacher: Very mean, okay. Roslyn? R: Rude Teacher: Rude. Katrina?
RESPONSES		
Revoice	Teacher repeats or rephrases what a student said	Student: Gloria is copying Officer Buckle. Teacher: Gloria is copying Officer Buckle. Student: The right thing. Teacher: She's doing the right thing.
Annotating	Teacher provides information that is not in the text	*Prevent* means not to happen.
Praise	Teacher agrees with, praises, or marks student response as important	Good. Excellent!
Recapping	Teacher sums up what has happened in the text	Okay, let's think about what we know. We know they had the biggest accident ever.
Agree	Teacher agrees with student	Yeah, pretty much.

Analyzing the Results

Maureen noticed several important differences in the initial queries, follow-up queries, and follow-up responses between the two discussions. Samples from Maureen's transcripts are in Table 4.4.

Initial Queries

Analyzing the initial queries, Maureen wrote, "Perhaps the most significant difference I noticed between the two approaches [basal versus *Text Talk*] was that the basal questions promoted personal inferences. Using the *Text Talk* model, I created queries that promoted text-based inferences, supporting students' understanding of the text."

Table 4.3 Maureen's Codes for Student Responses

Code	Explanation	Example
Correct	Complete and correct answer	Teacher: What's happening? (Gloria and the audience are falling asleep.) Student: They're bored and the dog is too.
Incomplete	May be correct, but not complete enough to judge, or is correct, but does not address entire question	Text: "Then one day, a television news team videotaped Officer Buckle in the state-college auditorium." Teacher: Why might they want to make a videotape? What might they do with it? Student: They might put it on video.
Incorrect	Incorrect answer	Teacher (following up on student's incomplete response above): For what? Student: For little kids who haven't seen it yet. So if they've seen it at their house, they didn't come to their school, they'll know all the safety tips.

Figure 4.1 Maureen's Initial Questions Using the Basal and *Text Talk* Models. Refer to Table 4.1 for explanation of categories.

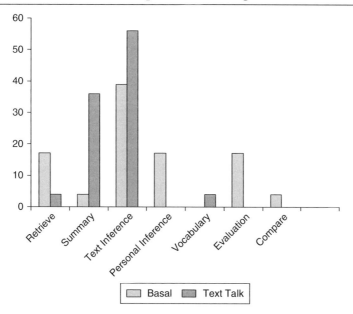

Figure 4.2 Maureen's Follow-Up Queries for Basal and *Text Talk* Plans. Refer to Table 4.2 for explanation of categories.

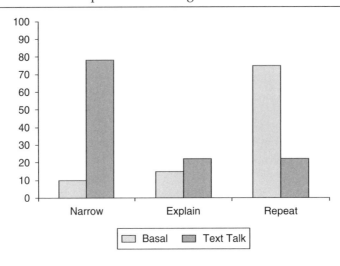

Figure 4.3 Maureen's Follow-Up Responses, Basal Versus *Text Talk*. See Table 4.2 for explanation of categories.

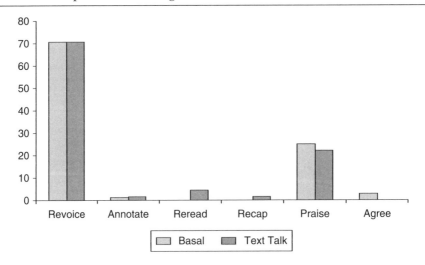

With the majority of the initial queries she prepared for *Text Talk* (92 percent), Maureen was asking students to make text-based inferences or to summarize the text, promoting language use and higher-level thinking. Although she also asked students to make text-based inferences with the basal questions (39 percent), she fairly equally asked them to retrieve information or to respond based on their own personal experience (34 percent). These retrieval and personal experience questions did not help Maureen understand whether students actually understood the story, nor did they promote the students discussing the text itself.

Table 4.4 Excerpts From Basal and *Text Talk* Transcripts

Basal Reader Transcript
Ruby the Copycat **(Rathman, 1991)**
(Text is in italics)

Monday was Ruby's first day in Miss Hart's class. "Class, this is Ruby," announced Miss Hart. "Ruby, you may use the empty desk behind Angela. Angela is the girl with the pretty red bow in her hair." Angela smiled at Ruby. Ruby smiled at Angela's bow and tiptoed to her seat. . . . "Class, please take out your reading books," said Miss Hart.

Teacher: Boys and girls, who are the main characters in the story?

Student 1: Ruby and Angela.

Teacher: Okay. Do you think there are any other main characters in the story?

Student 2: Mrs. Hart.

Teacher: Good. What is special about this day for Ruby?

Student 3: It's her first day in the school.

Teacher: It's her first day in the school. Does anyone have anything to add?

Teacher: One more question—How do you think Ruby feels on her first day?

Student 4: She feels shy.

Teacher: Maybe shy? [Student 5]?

Student 5: Mostly I guess happy.

Teacher: Happy, mostly. [Student 6]?

Student 6: Nervous.

Teacher: Nervous. [Student 7], what do you think?

Student 7: Maybe want to copycat?

Teacher: Maybe she wants to copycat? Good prediction. How would you feel on the first day of school? How would you feel on the first day of school? [Student 8]?

Student 8: Shy.

Teacher: Shy. I would too. [Student 9]?

Student 9: I always feel sad or happy.

Teacher: Sad or happy. Why might you feel sad?

Student 9: Because I don't want to go to school because this year I thought my teacher was Miss — but it was Miss —.

Teacher: I bet you feel much better about that now! Much happier, now that you got to know Miss —. Student 10, how would you feel on your first day?

Student 10: Frightened because if I got something wrong everybody would laugh at me.

Teacher: Frightened that you would get something wrong and people would laugh at you. Good and I only have time for one more. [Student 11], how would you feel on your first day of school?

Student 11: Shy.

Teacher: Shy, okay. Great.

(Continued)

Table 4.4 (Continued)

Text Talk **Transcript**

Officer Buckle and Gloria **(Rathman, 1995)**

(Text is in italics)

Then one day, a television news team videotaped Officer Buckle in the state-college auditorium.

Teacher: Boys and girls, what's going on?

Student 1: They are taking photographs of them.

Teacher: Okay, listen again.

REREADS: *Then one day, a television news team videotaped Officer Buckle.*

Teacher: Are they taking photographs, [Student 1]?

Student 1: No.

Teacher: What are they doing?

Student 1: Some news people are coming to take videos of them.

Teacher: They are taking a video. Why might they be taking a videotape of him?

Student 1: Because he's gonna be . . . (Inaudible)

Teacher: They're taking a videotape of the safety speech so it is both of them. Why might they want to take a videotape? What might they do with it? [Student 2]?

Student 2: They might put it on video.

Teacher: For what?

Student 2: For little kids who haven't seen it yet. So if they've seen it at their house, they didn't come to their school, they'll know all the safety tips.

Teacher: Okay, so maybe they are making a videotape to sell to children so they can watch it at home. Why else might a *news team* want to take a video?

Student 3: To show the kids what to do when they go out trick or treating.

Teacher: The question is the news team came to take a videotape. Why might the news team want the videotape?

Student 4: Maybe to put it on TV.

Teacher: Maybe they are going to put it on TV. Okay, let's find out.

Student Responses

Because there were differences in the initial questions, Maureen noticed a difference in the students' responses (see Figure 4.4). She wrote, "Because the majority of basal questions were personal inferences, a lot of them didn't necessarily have a right or wrong answer. A question like, 'How do you think Ruby feels on her first day?' can be answered and supported in a variety of ways—nervous, happy, sad, etc. Perhaps because of this, students' answers to basal questions were almost always correct. With the majority of my *Text Talk* questions, I asked students to summarize or make inferences, but students often simply recalled the story events. They gave incorrect or incomplete responses more often than with the basal text. That tells me the students were not familiar with this type of questioning."

Follow-Up Queries

The follow-up queries and questions were a little more revealing. Because many of the basal questions drew on personal experience, Maureen's pattern of responding was simply to ask another child the same question to collect more responses (72 percent of her follow-up questions), even though the first child answered the question correctly. Once she had saturated one question, she moved on. There was no connection from one question to the next. In contrast, Maureen planned her initial *Text Talk* queries to elicit text-based inferences or to have students summarize; therefore, most of her follow-up queries (40 percent) were used to ask students to explain the information they provided or to bring their more literal answers to an inference (28 percent). Maureen spent roughly three-quarters of her follow-up questions in the basal discussion collecting answers to repeated questions but not doing anything with them; she spent roughly three-quarters of her follow-ups in the *Text Talk* discussion having students build on responses to get at deeper levels of meaning.

Figure 4.4 Student Responses: Basal Versus *Text Talk*

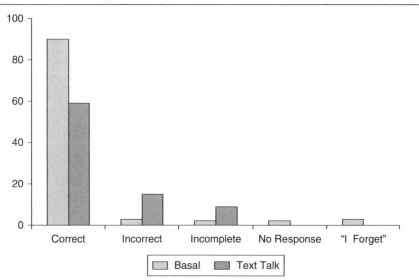

Follow-Up Responses

Even though her responses to students were not queries or questions, Maureen felt it was important to see how she was talking to students. Looking at her responses to them, Maureen noticed some things she was not pleased with. First, in both discussions, she continually repeated what students said—approximately 70 percent of her responses. She was pleased to see that she often reinforced students' participation and answers through praise but was dismayed that she never marked the response. In other words, she never said what, specifically, was "good," or what was "excellent."

Step 7: Maureen Reflects on the Data and What It Means.

When looking at your own practice, you might not be happy with what you see. Maureen found this out with her research. She reflected, "It was awful listening to myself conduct these discussions. I was surprised by how much I repeat what the students say. Why do I do this? Maybe I don't know what else to say? I don't know. But it's a terrible habit. I can see if I want other students to hear, or want to make a point, but I do it almost every time a student responds. That, combined with how I just ask someone else the same question I had already asked was so discouraging!"

Although Maureen found a lot of fault with her discussions, she used her transcripts as an opportunity to think about the questioning models (basal versus *Text Talk*), and how these influenced her practice. She wrote, "The *Text Talk* model emphasizes really thinking about the text—the big ideas and possible misunderstandings. After doing that, you need to segment the text at these specific points and develop queries that help students create meaning. On the other hand, the basal manual simply presented a series of four to six questions grouped together for every three or four pages of text. I didn't feel that the text was segmented appropriately, and stopping points were not clearly marked.

"While I was reading, I noticed that I needed to rephrase questions during both discussions, but for different reasons. I had to rephrase or repeat basal questions because they were sometimes long and confusing. I repeated or rephrased *Text Talk* queries to encourage deeper thinking and support clarification.

"The basal manual did not provide follow-up questions. I generated all follow-ups as I read the book. On the other hand, I developed follow-up queries for the *Text Talk* discussion in advance by predicting points of possible confusion. My follow-up queries really provided the scaffolding necessary for students to make several inter-textual leaps."

Step 8: Maureen Creates an Action Plan.

Maureen learned a lot about read-aloud discussions and her role as a facilitator. Her action plan included using what she learned to better her practice and some general suggestions for herself and others. Here are her suggestions:

"First and foremost, I should approach the basal series with a grain of salt and be skeptical of the quality of comprehension questions provided. . . . I need to evaluate whether or not the questions support student understanding of the text. The intent of questions should be to scaffold students to construct meaning from the text. When the goal is to teach comprehension strategies, the big idea of the text should be the main focus. Responding to literature by making text-to-life connections is important to the reading process . . . but there has to be a healthy balance between constructing meaning by focusing on the text itself, and encouraging personal anecdotes.

"Second, planning is so important. Much of the critical work takes place even before the read-aloud begins. [I should] develop queries that not only help students construct meaning, but also that are phrased so students understand what is being asked of them. Asking a long question with two or three parts will most likely lead to confusion. This practice discourages student response because they are not clear about the question.

"Third, planning a successful read-aloud experience, one that encourages students to construct meaning from the text, requires . . . more than prepar[ing] good questions. [I have to] be prepared to listen to what students say and respond appropriately. If students demonstrate a lack of understanding, [I can ask] well-thought follow-up queries to scaffold their comprehension.

"Last, one caution I would give to other teachers trying a more focused and planned discussion: Elaborate and insightful responses don't necessarily come easily or automatically to students. High-level questions require students to apply, analyze, integrate, and create using complex thinking processes. It's hard work! Therefore, students might be wrong as much as they are right. But don't revert back to easier questions! Teach students to make inferences so they can learn how to interpret text. The more students are exposed to this type of questioning, the more comfortable they will feel."

WRAP UP

Maureen's project captured some important facets of classroom research and literacy teaching and learning. It showed us how to look in depth at one small part of our practice. It is a lot of work to transcribe and analyze practice, but what Maureen gained from it was invaluable. Her reflection reinforces that looking at our own practice is hard, but ultimately very helpful. It is not easy to facilitate a good discussion. It requires planning and patience.

There are several take-home messages from Maureen's project for literacy teaching and learning. Comprehending text is hard. Students really need to work at it. Inferring does not necessarily come naturally. If we do not ask the right kinds of questions—queries—we might not know that students are experiencing difficulty. If Maureen had kept on with the basal questions, she may not have realized that the students could not take two pieces of text and come up with an inference. We need to create opportunities for students to make inter-textual inferences—inferences that require them to pull pieces of the text together.

In using discussion to support comprehension, the way we present queries and follow-ups to scaffold students' thinking really does matter. Discussion is an important part of learning, and how we conduct discussions influences students' comprehension.

HOW DOES MAUREEN'S PROJECT RELATE TO YOU?

Discussion is a key component in any classroom. In that way, it is easy to envision any teacher from preschool through college thinking about doing what Maureen did—working to refine discussion practices. You might want to begin simply by keeping track of the kinds of questions you ask students, and how they respond. Correct responses may not always signal full comprehension. Rather, as Maureen learned, maybe your questions do not promote enough higher-level thinking. All teachers can think about what they ask, how students respond, and how they then follow-up on that response.

Regardless of your subject matter, the text practices you read about in this chapter easily apply to you. Students need to read text in every school subject. Maureen learned a lot about thinking about the text, segmenting it into important discussion units, and posing thoughtful queries. This process is not limited to storybooks. In fact, the initial work from which *Text Talk* came, *Questioning the Author* (Beck, McKeown, Hamilton, & Kucan, 1997), focused on reading and discussing social studies and science text in the upper elementary grades.

YOU TRY IT

You have two tasks to try—one to learn about classroom research and one to learn about discussion and comprehension.

Classroom Research Task.

Go back to the staircase and questions you created after reading Chapter 2 and begin to plan out your own research. Plan your instruction for now.

Literacy Task.

Choose a piece of text that you and your students might read (any subject area). Make sure that the ideas in the text are really worth talking about—that they have some "meat" to them. If your text is a narrative text, follow the steps to create a *Text Talk* as presented in this chapter. If your text is an information text, jot down the main points you think the students should understand. Plan your stopping points, queries, and follow-ups. Try it out. If you are really interested in analyzing your practice, do what Maureen did—audiotape and transcribe.

5

Keeping Track of Assessment Data Makes Teaching Easier

Classroom Research Spotlight
Step 5: Implement the Plan and Collect Data
(Implementing Logistics: Organizing Data)

Literacy Spotlights
Early Literacy
Using Data to Inform Literacy Instruction

The purpose of assessment is to inform instruction. Yet, in the climate of accountability, teachers find it difficult to keep up with the sheer volume of assessments. Keeping track of data is the first step in using that data to inform instruction. In this chapter, we will look at how Jessica, a first-grade teacher in a large, urban school district, used classroom research to analyze the skills the district-mandated assessments were measuring, choose assessments that would fill in assessment gaps, and develop a system to pull the information together to help inform her instruction.

JESSICA'S RESEARCH

Context for Jessica's Project.

Jessica teaches first grade at a K–5 elementary school within a large, urban school district. The student population is predominantly Hispanic, although many ethnic groups are also represented. Twenty-five percent of the students receive English as a Second Language (ESL) services. Most of the students are from low-income families—83 percent of the school's students are eligible for free or reduced-price lunch. The school is classified as "low performing and not improving." Jessica's classroom includes twenty-six students, twenty-four of whose parents gave permission for her to share their data: fourteen boys and ten girls. Fifteen of the students attended kindergarten at Jessica's school. The remaining nine came from other schools within or outside the district.

Step 1: Jessica Notices a Problem in Using Data.

Jessica had been thinking about how she was determining her students' needs in literacy and using that information to inform her literacy teaching. She wrote, "In the past I have not made effective use of assessments and notes about my students' progress to track their progress across the year. I have also not used the information to really tailor my instruction to my students' needs. With the new assessments and collections of work samples now required by my district, I really need to develop a better system for organizing and summarizing all of this data in terms of what it means for my students."

Step 2: Jessica Inquires Into First-Grade Requirements.

To begin organizing her students' data effectively, Jessica had to determine what they were expected to do. She needed to investigate her district's expectations for first grade, its curriculum, and its assessments.

What Should First Graders Know?

Jessica first investigated the literacy standards her district was using. Here's what she found: "The standards suggest that students should enter first grade reading on levels A, B, or C, and exit reading on levels I or J, according to Guided Reading levels (Fountas & Pinnell, 1996). Students should be able to separate and blend phonemes such as in the word *cat* (/c/-/a/-/t/). They should know the regular letter-sound correspondences and use them to figure out regularly spelled one- and two-syllable words, and represent these sounds in writing."

Jessica found a great deal of research stressing the importance of the print-sound code, and specifically that the alphabetic principle and phonological awareness are determining factors of future reading achievement (Bond & Dykstra, 1997).

What Does My District Expect of Teachers and Students?

Jessica also investigated what her district expects of students. Here is what she found: "My school district is in its third year of using [standards] as benchmarks of student progress. Data from the School Accountability for Learning and Teaching (SALT) survey (http://www.infoworks.ride.uri.edu), collected in all districts in my state, shows that student achievement has improved at my school in the years since we have been using the standards, but most students are still achieving below the standard in reading and writing.

"My district adopted a balanced literacy framework simultaneously with the standards [which] incorporates many literacy components (read aloud, independent reading, guided reading, shared reading, word work, interactive writing, and writing workshop). Although there are separate instructional periods (a read-aloud block, a writing workshop block, etc.), the framework stresses the interconnectedness of these components, so that there are many opportunities to give systematic, explicit instruction in phonemic awareness, the alphabetic principle, concepts about print, decoding, fluency, comprehension strategies, and writing skills throughout the day. I am required to collect student work samples to document progress within each of these components.

"My district adopted the *Developmental Reading Assessment* (DRA) (Beaver, 2001), [and] several tasks to supplement the DRA, including a writing sample; two running records analyzed for accuracy, fluency, and comprehension; sight word knowledge; anecdotal records noting phonemic awareness; word recognition; reading behaviors; and a spelling assessment."

How Are the Standards, Curriculum, and Assessments Aligned?

Jessica found that although the mandated assessments addressed most of the standards, there were gaps. Additionally, she did not know how to take "anecdotal records" that would reliably capture students' current skills in phonemic awareness and phonics.

Step 3: Jessica Develops Specific Questions.

Jessica felt she still needed to think about the assessment gaps. She also felt if she could organize her data better, she would understand her students better and provide more targeted instruction, which would lead to student growth. Therefore, her classroom research questions are mainly teacher-as-learner questions.

Teacher-as-Learner Questions
What supplemental assessments can I give that will help me to see where my students are in their progression toward meeting the standards?
How can I efficiently summarize and make use of the assessment data that I gather on my twenty-six students in order to see trends and patterns for each student and the class as a whole "at a glance"?

Student Learning Question
What will the data tell me about what my students need to know?

Step 4: Jessica Formulates a Plan.

Planning Data Collection

The first step in Jessica's plan was to decide what additional information she needed about her students. She wrote, "I knew from analyzing our mandated assessments that we were not assessing phonics, phonemic awareness, or spelling in a systematic, developmental way." Jessica identified assessments that would fill this gap:

- The Yopp Phonemic Awareness Assessment (1995), which assesses rhyme recognition, phoneme isolation, and phoneme blending
- The Letter Identification task of *An Observation Survey* (Clay, 1998), which assesses any or all of letter names, letter sounds, and key word knowledge
- The *Primary Spelling Inventory* (Bear, Invernizzi, Templeton, & Johnston, 2003), which assesses students' ability to use sound/symbol knowledge to represent words in print

Jessica used each of these assessments in addition to the *Developmental Reading Assessment* required by the district to assess her students' literacy skills.

Planning Logistics: How to Organize the Data

Keeping student data in individual folders was not working. Jessica wanted to be able to view her assessment data "at a glance." She designed spreadsheets for summarizing and analyzing student assessment results. (You can easily design these using Excel or a similar spreadsheet program.)

Planning Instruction

Although Jessica's district had a balanced literacy framework, they did not have materials or programs that helped teachers plan how to systematically incorporate phonics and phonemic awareness skills. Jessica provided instruction daily through morning messages and the other literacy areas, but she felt she was just picking and choosing what to teach. In addition to getting the assessments and spreadsheets ready, Jessica wanted to choose resources that would help her plan phonemic awareness and phonics instruction, based on students' needs. Here is what she chose to help herself:

- *Phonics A to Z* (Blevins, 1998)
- *Month-by-Month Phonics* (Cunningham & Hall, 1997)
- Word Building (Beck, 1999)
- The Hampton-Brown Phonics program (Kratky, 2000) (recently purchased by Jessica's district, but not yet in use)

Step 5: Jessica Implements Her Plan and Collects Data.

Jessica's goal was Step 6 in the classroom research cycle: Analyze and Make Sense of the Data. However, I spotlighted Step 5, Implement, because this is what gave Jessica the needed information to reach her goal.

Logistics

In order for Jessica to accomplish what she wanted to accomplish, she needed to use her time wisely. She noted, "September is an important time for assessing students and developing classroom routines and expectations. I realized that if I spent most of those fragile days sitting one-on-one assessing students, I might miss out on valuable time for setting a positive tone and clear expectations for the year. . . . [I needed to make] administrative choices [that would give] me the time that I needed to teach, circulate, and reinforce positive work habits around the classroom."

One of Jessica's administrative decisions was training a teaching assistant to administer the letter identification task (Clay, 1998). Additionally, because of the time needed to administer the DRA (approximately twenty minutes per student), Jessica decided to get students' end-of-year DRA results from their kindergarten teachers for those students who attended her school in kindergarten (fifteen students) and give the DRA only to those students for whom the records were not available. Jessica's assessment plan is in Table 5.1.

The teaching assistant completed the letter assessment with each student. Jessica then administered the phonemic awareness assessment (Yopp, 1995) individually to each student, the *Primary Spelling Inventory* (Bear et al., 2003) in small groups, and the DRA only to the nine students who had not been assessed in kindergarten. After Jessica completed each assessment, she entered the results on the spreadsheet she had designed (see Tables 5.2

Table 5.1 Jessica's Assessment Plan

Assessment	Which Students? How Given?	Who Administers?
1. Letter Name and Sound Identification	All students Individually	Teaching Assistant
2. Phonemic Awareness	All students Individually	Jessica
3. *Primary Spelling Inventory*	All students Small groups	Jessica
4. *Developmental Reading Assessment* (DRA)	Students who were not assessed at the end of kindergarten Individually	Jessica

through 5.5). She then went through and highlighted scores that fell below the end of kindergarten or begining of first-grade benchmarks.

Choosing her assessments, designing her spreadsheets, administering the tasks, recording the information, and highlighting areas of need paved the way for Jessica to look at her students' literacy development. The spreadsheets she created served two purposes. First, she could look across the rows to see needs of each individual student. Second, she could look down the columns to see "at a glance" trends in the needs of small groups or the whole class. Additionally, by creating the spreadsheets in a data program like Excel, Jessica could sort the data to help think about instruction. She sorted the charts included here in ascending order (students most in need to students least in need).

Step 6: Jessica Analyzes the Data.

Looking at the summary chart for the letter identification task (see Table 5.2), Jessica noted that she did not need to spend a great deal of whole class time teaching beginning consonants. Her students had this knowledge already. She could begin to focus on short vowels.

Analyzing the summary chart for the phonemic awareness assessment (see Table 5.3), Jessica noticed that ten of her beginning first graders fell below the kindergarten mean on the rhyme identification task. Her students' ability to isolate sounds in words was mixed. Just as her students knew the letter and sound correspondences of consonants, they could, by and large, separate the beginning and ending consonant sounds from words (for example, "What's the first sound you hear in *boy*?"). Many students had difficulty identifying the middle sounds in words ("What sound do you hear in the middle of the word, *cat*?"), which were typically vowel sounds. However, going back to the standards, Jessica saw that this is a target skill for the *end* of first grade. Twelve of Jessica's twenty-four students had difficulty blending two phonemes in simple words (/*i*/-/*s*/ = *is*, /*ee*/-/*t*/ = *eat*) or the onset and rime of one-syllable words (/*d*/-/*og*/ = *dog*, /*m*/-/*an*/ = *man*), which six-year-olds should be able to do (Moats, 2000).

Jessica found similar results on the *Primary Spelling Inventory*. Overall, her students used appropriate beginning and ending sounds in their spelling, and many included a vowel in the middle of their words, indicating that they were aware of medial sounds in simple words. Looking further at the spreadsheet, Jessica noticed clusters of different skills, so she sorted the data by spelling stage (see Table 5.4). She identified three distinct groups of students: early letter-name-alphabetic spellers who need to work on beginning and ending consonant sounds, middle letter-name-alphabetic spellers who consistently use but confuse short vowels, and late letter-name-alphabetic spellers who have a good grasp on short vowels and are ready for digraphs and blends. She also had one student who was at the beginning within word pattern stage.

With the DRA spreadsheet, Jessica noticed that all of her students were achieving at or above the expected levels for entering first grade. She also

Table 5.2 Example of Jessica's Letter-Sound Identification Chart

Student #	Total Score Total Possible Score = 54			Aa			Ff			Kk		
	Name	Sound	Word	Name	Sound	Word	Name	Sound	Word	Name	Sound	Word
1	41	19	26	xxx	xxx	xxx				xx		
2	44	32	44	xxx	xxx	xxx	xx	xx	xx	xx	xx	xx
3	45	27	35	xxx	xx	xxx	xx	xx	xx	xx	xx	xx
4	46	41	45	xxx	xxx	xxx	xx	xx	xx		xx	xx
5	49	0	28	xxx		xxx	xx			xx		xx
6	50	49	49	xxx	xxx	xxx	xx	xx	xx	xx	xx	xx
7	50	52	51	xxx	xx	xx	xx	xx	xx	xx	xx	xx
8	52	50	48	xxx	xxx	xxx	xx	xx	x	xx	xx	xx
9	52	48	51	xxx	xx	xx	xx	xx	xx	xx	xx	xx
10	52	52	52	xxx	xx	xx	xx	xx	xx	xx	xx	xx
11	53	53	52	xxx	xx	xx	xx	xx	xx	xx	xx	xx
12	53	15	38	xxx	xxx	xx	xx	xx	x	xx	xx	x

(Continued)

Table 5.2 (Continued)

Student #	Total Score (Total Possible Score = 54)			Aa			Ff			Kk		
	Name	Sound	Word	Name	Sound	Word	Name	Sound	Word	Name	Sound	Word
13	53	53	53	xxx	xx	xx	xx	xx	xx	xx	xx	xx
14	53	51	51	xxx	xx	xx	xx	xx	xx	xx	xx	xx
15	53	53	53	xxx	xx	xx	xx	xx	xx	xx	xx	xx
16	53	52	40	xxx	xxx	xxx	xx	xx	xx	xx	xx	xx
17	53	51	53	xxx	xx	xx	xx	xx	xx	xx	xx	xx
18	53	49	52	xxx	xx	xx	xx	xx	xx	xx	xx	xx
19	53	53	53	xxx	xx	xx	xx	xx	xx	xx	xx	xx
20	53	53	53	xxx	xx	xx	xx	xx	xx	xx	xx	xx
21	54	54	52	xxx	xx	xx	xx	xx	xx	xx	xx	xx
22	54	54	52	xxx	xx	xx	xx	xx	xx	xx	xx	xx
23	54	54	50	xxx	xxx	xxx	xx	xx	xx	xx	xx	xx
24	54	54	53	xxx	xx	xx	xx	xx	xx	xx	xx	xx

Table 5.3 Phonemic Awareness Results, September

	Rhyming	Isolating Sounds				Blending			
	Score	Total	Beginning Sound	Middle Sound	End Sound	Total	Two Sounds	Onset/Rime	3-4 Sounds
K Mean	15/20	9/15	(5 total)	(5 total)	(5 total)	20/30	(10 total)	(10 total)	(10 total)
Student #									
3	8	1	1	0	0	9	9	0	0
17	9	12	4	4	4	18	10	5	3
4	9	12	5	2	5	20	10	6	4
12	10	3	1	0	2	4	3	1	0
5	10	0	0	0	0	0	0	0	0
1	12	3	1	0	2	2	2	0	0
19	12	11	4	3	4	16	10	5	1
15	13	8	1	2	5	25	10	9	6
11	14	7	0	2	5	26	10	8	8
2	14	9	5	1	3	16	10	6	0
23	17	11	5	2	4	19	9	7	3
7	18	12	5	2	5	22	9	9	4

(Continued)

Table 5.3 (Continued)

	Rhyming	Isolating Sounds				Blending			
	Score	Total	Beginning Sound	Middle Sound	End Sound	Total	Two Sounds	Onset/Rime	3-4 Sounds
K Mean	15/20	9/15	(5 total)	(5 total)	(5 total)	20/30	(10 total)	(10 total)	(10 total)
Student #									
6	19	14	5	5	4	16	8	8	0
21	19	14	4	5	5	25	10	8	7
8	19	10	5	0	5	18	9	6	3
13	19	14	5	4	5	25	10	10	5
14	19	13	5	3	5	24	10	7	7
20	19	10	5	0	5	17	10	7	1
22	20	14	5	4	5	24	10	9	5
9	20	10	4	2	4	26	10	8	8
16	20	10	5	0	5	29	10	10	9
10	20	13	5	3	5	28	10	10	8
18	20	12	4	4	4	25	10	10	8
24	20	10	5	0	5	3	3	0	0

Table 5.4 Primary Spelling Inventory, October

Student #		Consonants		Short Vowels	Digraphs and Blends	Long Vowel Patterns	Other Vowel Patterns	Syllable Junctures, etc.
		Initial	Final					
Possible Points	62	6	6	7	21	8	8	8
1	4	3	1	0	0	0	0	0
3	4	3	0	0	1	0	0	0
6	6	0	5	1	0	0	0	0
19	10	5	4	1	0	0	0	0
4	13	5	6	1	1	0	0	0
5	13	6	6	1	0	0	0	0
8	13	6	6	1	0	0	0	0
10	13	6	6	1	0	0	0	0
12	13	6	5	2	0	0	0	0
14	13	6	6	1	0	0	0	0
20	13	6	6	1	0	0	0	0
24	13	6	6	1	0	0	0	0

(Continued)

Table 5.4 (Continued)

Student #	Possible Points	Consonants		Short Vowels	Digraphs and Blends	Long Vowel Patterns	Other Vowel Patterns	Syllable Junctures, etc.
		Initial	Final					
Possible Points	62	6	6	7	21	8	8	8
2	14	6	6	2	0	0	0	0
17	15	6	6	2	1	0	0	0
18	15	6	6	2	1	0	0	0
6	16	6	6	4	0	0	0	0
16	16	6	6	3	1	0	0	0
7	18	6	6	6	0	0	0	0
15	20	6	6	6	1	1	0	0
9	21	6	6	7	2	0	0	0
22	26	6	6	5	7	0	1	1
13	33	6	6	7	12	0	0	2
11	36	6	6	7	12	0	3	2
21	51	6	6	7	20	5	4	3

NOTES:

Indicates need

Indicates exceeding expectations

Table 5.5 DRA Results, End K or Begin Grade 1

Independent Reading Level	Student #	Book Selection	Reads Familiar Text	Accuracy	Previews	Connects/ Predicts	Fluency	Intonation	Strategies	Self-Corrects
2	1	2	2	2						
2	2	3	3	2	4	4	3	4	3	3
2	3	2	2	2	2	2	2	2	2	2
2	5	2	2	2			2			
2	8	2	2	2						
2	12	1	1	2						
3	4	4	3	3	3	3	5	5	4	3
3	6	3	3	3	3	3	4	4	3	3
3	7	4	4	3	4	3	5	5	6	6
3	9	4	3	3	4		6	6		
3	15	4	3	3	3	3	4	4	4	3
3	19	4	4	3	4	3	4	4	4	4
3	20	4	5	3	5	5	3	4	4	3

(Continued)

Table 5.5 (Continued)

Independent Reading Level	Student #	Book Selection	Reads Familiar Text	Accuracy	Previews	Connects/ Predicts	Fluency	Intonation	Strategies	Self-Corrects
3	24	4	4	3	4	3	4	3		
4	10	4	4	3	4	3	6	6	5	4
4	13	4	4	3	5	5	6	6	5	3
4	14	4	4	3	5	5	6	6	5	8
4	16	4	4	3	4	3	4	5	5	
4	17	4	5	3	5	4	3	4		
4	18	4	4	3	4	3	4	4	4	4
4	22	3	5	3	5	3	7	5	5	6
6	11	5	5	3	5	5	5	5	4	4
6	23	5	5	3	4	5	6	5		
12	21	6	6	5	5	5	7	5		

Note: The number (1–8) under each heading represents the student's developmental level on that skill based on the DRA Continuum. These numbers correspond generally to reading development as follows: 1–2 = Emergent Reader, 3–4 = Early Reader, 5–6 = Transitional Reader, 7–8 = Self-Extending Reader. Beginning first graders are typically emergent-early readers.

noticed that the students were performing at or above their respective levels in all areas measured by the DRA as listed on the horizontal headings of the matrix (see Table 5.5).

After analyzing each spreadsheet, Jessica developed a whole-class profile of strengths and needs. Once she understood her class as a whole, she went back through her matrices to look for students who showed particular patterns across the tasks. To make this easy, she sorted each chart by student. She found four students (Students 1, 3, 4, and 5) who were consistently challenged across every task, and an additional two students (Students 6 and 8) who struggled on most tasks.

Step 7: Jessica Reflects on Her Data and How They Inform District Mandates.

Jessica needed to think about whether the time she put into organizing her data was worthwhile and what her data told her about the district's assessment requirements. She reflected: "I found the matrices very helpful on two levels. First, I was able to see where each student was in relation to the standards. Second, I was also able to gain an "at a glance" look at the skills and needs of my class as a whole. The combined results of the alphabetic knowledge, phonemic awareness, primary spelling inventory, and DRA assessments gave me information to adjust my instruction for particular individuals, small groups, and the whole class throughout many of the balanced literacy components as well."

With respect to what her district required of her as a first-grade teacher, Jessica wrote, "Most of the assessments that I administered for this research were based on what my district would like to see, but I felt that some of the [district's] required assessments and work samples were too vague to yield useful results. I reflected on how I could choose assessments that would be the most informative to me, based on research and staying within the guidelines of the instructional framework in my district. This is the first time I have taken the time to think about what more information I may want to obtain beyond what is required. It has proven to be very useful to me. I know a great deal more about my students' literacy skills base than ever before."

Step 8: Jessica Creates an Action Plan.

Jessica's follow-up took two paths—immediate and future.

Immediate

Based on her data analysis, Jessica planned for whole class, individual, and small group instruction using instructional strategies she found in the teaching resources she identified. First, she provided extra instruction and practice in letter-sound relationships through games, picture sorts, and alphabet linking charts or sound boards (Bear et al., 2003) in small group and one-on-one sessions to students who needed this extra instruction.

Second, Jessica planned phonemic awareness activities based on what groups of students needed. She incorporated many rhyming songs during transitions, read and made innovations for poems that had rhymes, and played rhyming games during center time. She helped students isolate sounds in words using sound boxes (Elkonin boxes) and sound box activities suggested in her district's phonics program. She used transition times to sing songs and play phoneme blending games, just as she had done with alphabetic knowledge and rhyming. Because Jessica had three students who struggled across all areas, she targeted them to receive intensive small group and one-on-one instruction throughout the year.

Jessica continually used her spreadsheets for reference. She wrote, "I keep the summary sheets in my plan book so that I can easily access information about student skills and note the amount of time I need to spend and the format I need to use in teaching specific skills or lessons suggested by the word work, shared reading, and guided reading resource books I chose."

Future

First, Jessica's data clearly showed her that teaching one word-work program to the whole class simultaneously would be insufficient given the range of her students' knowledge. However, with a fifteen-minute word-work block built into each day, she remained unsure how to address the needs of all students. She felt that the majority of her students needed the skills taught in the standard curriculum used in her district, which works out great for them, but there are some who fall a bit below and others a bit above that skills base. She realized she will need to continue to investigate ways to differentiate her word-work block to meet the needs of all students.

Second, Jessica has concerns about her system in general. Here are her pieces of advice and some questions.

"Finding the most useful assessments, administering them, organizing the results, and making subsequent instructional decisions is very time consuming. I'm glad that I made the time to find assessments that are useful to me, and developed systems for effectively summarizing the information I gained. But, it was incredibly time consuming. Despite this, I believe that this method of assessment, review, analysis, and planning is worthy of trying for a few more years in order to work toward greater efficiency.

"I still haven't figured out how to effectively monitor and keep track of student progress. I know I need to maintain and analyze records of students' reading habits, skills, and strategies on a regular basis, not just biannually. But I still have so many questions: How can I continue to monitor student progress during times when assessments are not required? How often should I formally collect data using the letter identification, phonemic awareness, and spelling inventory assessments? Which assessments could I adapt and embed directly into daily lessons and activities instead of pulling kids out?"

Current

Jessica has since moved from her first-grade classroom to a position as literacy coach in her building. She spends a lot of her time teaching teachers and principals how to use assessment data to inform instruction. Since she conducted her research, her school has increased along several important dimensions—there are more Hispanic students (57 percent) and more families eligible for free or reduced-price lunch (89 percent), and the English Language Arts (ELA) achievement has improved. As of this writing, the school changed classification to "in need of improvement and making progress." Contributing to the increased achievement is Jessica's push to help teachers navigate mandates and use data to inform instruction, which she learned through her research. Using data and carefully monitoring student progress has been a significant factor in raising student achievement.

WRAP UP

There are several take-home messages about classroom research from Jessica's project. First, it is possible to conduct classroom research even in districts that have particular mandated instruction or assessments. Jessica followed what her district required, yet still investigated what she thought was missing, and took the steps necessary to fill in the gaps and organize information for herself. Additionally, Jessica began her project to help herself navigate *through* the mandates, not around them. She was required to give many assessments, yet had not really had professional development focused on how to organize and use the data to inform instruction. Her project helped her to teach herself how to do this.

With respect to literacy teaching and learning, Jessica's project gives us insight into what beginning reading skills to assess and provides ideas on how to assess them. Letter names are important, but letter sounds may be more important in beginning reading. Assessing phonemic awareness in a more structured way provides more helpful information for instruction than does keeping anecdotal notes. Spelling is a great window into both students' sound-symbol knowledge and their phonemic awareness.

HOW DOES JESSICA'S PROJECT RELATE TO YOU?

Although the topic of beginning reading might not relate to you, how Jessica went about creating a system to organize and use her data *does* relate to you if you work in a school in this current climate of accountability. Every teacher in every school gathers some type of student data. Are you using your data effectively and efficiently? If not, Jessica's ideas might help you organize the data you gather so that you can use it to inform your instruction.

YOU TRY IT

Your task from Chapter 4 was to begin to plan your research. To help you with this, and to help you connect the ideas you just read, you will organize your own data.

- Using the topic area you have chosen for your research, gather already existing student data about this area. For example, if you chose to investigate comprehension, gather whatever comprehension assessments you have given to your students. The assessments can be formal (a published test or mandated assessment) or informal (tests that you made, notes you have taken, etc.).
- Develop a way of organizing these data so that you can see your class as a whole and each student individually. Use Jessica's spreadsheets for ideas.
- Once you have organized your data, create a list of students' strengths and needs.
- Once you have your list, rethink your own idea for research. Is what you planned going to address those strengths and needs?

6

Differentiating Word Study Instruction

Classroom Research Spotlight
Step 4: Plan

Literacy Spotlight
Phonics and Word Study

Teaching phonics or word study is important for reading and writing development throughout the grades. In the early grades, teachers begin by teaching the basics—hearing sounds in words, identifying letters, and mapping letters to sounds. As children move up the grades, teachers focus on patterns within words, meaning units (prefixes, suffixes, roots), word meanings, multiple meanings, and other complex concepts. Oftentimes a teacher is required to use a particular curriculum that may not be appropriate for all students, or has trouble figuring out how to differentiate instruction based on students' current skills. In this chapter, we will look at how Jenn, a first-grade teacher, used classroom research to differentiate her word study instruction.

I have chosen to highlight Step 4 in this chapter: Planning. The only way to approach the complicated task of differentiating instruction is to have a clear plan for what you want to accomplish and how you can accomplish it.

JENN'S RESEARCH

Context for Jenn's Project.

Jenn teaches first grade in a White, middle-class, suburban school district. Although students' English language arts scores are good, the school is classified as "in need of improvement and making progress," because it is slightly below the state target for educating students with disabilities. Jenn teaches nineteen students, three of whom are not present during her daily two-and-a-half-hour literacy instruction period due to split placements with kindergarten or a special needs self-contained classroom.

Step 1: Jenn Observes Her Students and Her Practice.

During the fall Jenn had become frustrated with her classroom instruction. She wrote, "As a first-grade teacher, I strive to best meet the individual needs of my students. [Yet] many of the instructional materials and programs provided to our school are designed for whole-class instruction and do not seem to fit these individual needs, especially [for] the children who perform above or below [the] standards."

Step 2: Jenn Inquires Into Her Focus Area.

Like Jessica in the previous chapter, Jenn started her inquiry by turning to the state standards for her grade and to research on beginning reading. Here are the major points she discovered.

Grade Level Expectations for Grade 1

Our Grade 1 *Tri-State Grade Level Expectations* (for New Hampshire, Vermont, and Rhode Island, 2006, see http://www.ridoe.net/Instruction/gle.aspx) for phonemic awareness and phonics indicate that students should be competent in the following:

- Producing pairs of rhyming words
- Counting syllables in one- to four-syllable words
- Blending and segmenting syllables and onset-rime (e.g., cup-cake)
- Blending and segmenting phonemes in one-syllable words (e.g., f-i-sh)
- Isolating phonemes in single-syllable words
- Deleting phonemes in one-syllable words
- Sounding out regularly spelled (decodable) one- or two-syllable words using letter-sound correspondence knowledge
- Reading regularly spelled one- or two-syllable words using knowledge of sounds and letter patterns
- Reading grade-level appropriate words (in connected text)

"I Need to Teach Phonics and Word Study in a Systematic Way"

Wading through extensive research on word study instruction for beginning readers, Jenn noted a consistent theme—systematic phonics programs yield better results for young readers than non-systematic phonics, sight word, or meaning-based programs (National Reading Panel, 2000). Good beginning readers use a variety of decoding skills such as letter-sound associations and blending letters and sounds together (Foorman, Francis, Fletcher, & Schatschneider, 1998), as well as identifying words by analogy ("If I can read *cat* then I can read *sat*.") (Greany, Tunmer, & Chapman, 1997). Systematic phonics programs assist young readers in developing these decoding and word analysis skills.

"I Need to Teach Phonemic Awareness"

Jenn found that phoneme awareness—the understanding that words are made up of individual sounds—is also important to beginning reading and that teaching phonemic awareness helps early reading skills (Ball & Blachman, 1991). Teaching phonemic awareness helps children understand that the sounds in words can be separated (for example, the word *cat* can be separated into /c/-/a/-/t/) or that separate sounds can be blended together to make a word (for example, the sounds /c/-/a/-/t/ can be put together to make *cat*). Phonemic awareness and phonics can be taught together—it is actually beneficial to combine teaching phonemic awareness with teaching letter sounds and how to put the letters and sounds together in words (Fielding-Barnsley, 1997).

"What Program Should I Be Using?"

Jenn was not surprised to find that not all programs are equal with respect to how well they help students learn to read. She was surprised to find, however, that no one *systematic, structured* phonics program is better than another (National Reading Panel, 2000). The key is in the terms *systematic* and *structured*. Otherwise, the program does not really matter. Jenn then needed to determine what was considered "systematic" and "structured."

- *Systematic* means that the program has a planned sequence that moves from easier to harder in a predictable, developmental progression.
- *Structured* means that the teacher explicitly teaches the concepts and has students practice them in a variety of ways.

Knowing that all phonics programs are not the same means that teachers must be educated about how to evaluate different programs to determine which are based on strong evidence and how they can most effectively use these programs in their own classrooms (National Reading Panel, 2000).

"I Need to Differentiate Instruction"

Jenn found that early reading programs need decoding instruction that accommodates individual differences rather than being one-size-fits-all (Pressley, 2002). Additionally, she found that the most influential factors for student success are the importance teachers place on meeting individual needs and their attitudes toward changing practices. In an inclusive environment, students at all levels of understanding can learn more effectively when teachers adjust instruction for individual learning styles and needs (Hauslein & Kapusnick, 2001). The goal of differentiation is using continuous assessment to provide instruction appropriate to each child's Zone of Proximal Development (Vygotsky, 1978).

Jenn's "A-ha"
If I use an integration of different early reading programs and their various strategies, I should be able to better meet my students' instructional needs.

Step 3: Jenn Develops Specific Questions.

After thinking about the issues around teaching word study, Jenn settled on the following questions:

Teacher-as-Learner Questions
Where are my students in their word study (phonics, phonemic awareness) development? How can I design an effective differentiated word study program for my students?

Student Learning Question
Will providing differentiated instruction help my students make gains in reading?

Step 4: Jenn Formulates a Plan.

Planning includes more than just selecting materials. Logistics were a big part of Jenn's planning.

Logistics

Choosing Assessments

Jenn wanted to assess her students' word study skills—phonics, phonemic awareness, and word reading. When she investigated her district's assessments, she realized that the district did not have any assessments of these skills. Jenn was in the position that many of us are in teaching—needing materials but having no budget to purchase them. She investigated assessments online and found one quick to administer, and free. Jenn wrote, "I chose to use the DIBELS [*Dynamic Indicators of Basic Early Literacy Skills*, (Good & Kaminski, 2002)] to assess my students. My district doesn't use this assessment, but it's quick and will give me the information I need to group my students."

Jenn administered three subtests of the DIBELS to each student individually: Phoneme Segmentation Fluency, Nonsense Word Fluency, and Oral Reading Fluency subtests. Each task takes one minute. Here is how each subtest works.

- Phoneme Segmentation Fluency: The teacher says a word and asks students to tell all the sounds in that word. (For example, "Tell me all the sounds you hear in the word *cat*."). The students receive one point for each sound segment identified within one minute. (They could get one point for "cat," two points for "/ca/-/t/," or "/c/-/at/," or three points for "c/-/a/-/t/").
- Nonsense Word Fluency: The teacher asks students to read two- and three-letter make-believe words the best they can. As in the Phoneme Segmentation Fluency, students receive one point for each sound or sound segment they correctly identify in one minute.
- Oral Reading Fluency: The teacher asks the student to read a passage out loud. The student receives one point for each word read correctly in one minute.

Grouping Students for Instruction

Once Jenn scored her students' assessments based on both the middle- and end-of-first-grade benchmarks (she began implementing her project in January), she categorized them according to the DIBELS recommendations (meets the benchmark, strategic instructional support needed, intensive instructional support needed). Based on the results and her knowledge of her students, Jenn created three groups for instruction.

- **Group 1**: Three students who were in the "intensive instructional support" category, and one student who was in the "strategic instructional support" category; this group typically performed below expectations on literacy tasks.
- **Group 2**: Six students who met or exceeded middle- but not end-of-first-grade benchmarks; these students typically met expectations on literacy tasks.
- **Group 3**: Six students who met or exceeded end-of-first-grade benchmarks; these students typically exceeded expectations on literacy tasks.

Choosing Instruction

Although Jenn's district did not mandate a particular program, it had recently purchased a program and strongly recommended its use. Jenn describes the district's efforts: "My district recently provided all primary teachers with professional development focused on *Guided Reading: Good First Teaching for All Children* (Fountas & Pinnell, 1996), which is geared toward small, flexible groups. The district also provided us *Phonics Lessons: Letters, Words, and How They Work: Grade 1* (Fountas & Pinnell, 2002), which is the companion word study portion of the *Guided Reading* program. *Phonics Lessons* is all-encompassing and designed for whole-class instruction, with practice activities in literacy centers. The program consists of 100 mini-lessons, assessment checklists, and a month-by-month planning guide encompassing early literacy concepts, high-frequency words, phonological and phonemic awareness, spelling patterns, letter knowledge, words structure, letter-sound relationships, word-solving actions, and word meaning."

Jenn was worried that *Phonics Lessons* would not be sequential and structured enough for her struggling students. Although the program contained lots of good ideas, Jenn felt it was overwhelming. It required too much work on her part to figure out how to sequence and structure the lessons for her struggling students. She researched several different programs to find good matches for each group. Jenn describes what she decided for each group.

Group 1: "Students in Group 1 experienced two areas of difficulty—weakness in phoneme segmentation ("How many sounds are in this word?") and decoding (reading the make-believe words). To help with phoneme awareness (including phoneme segmentation), I chose *Road to the Code* (Blachman, Ball, Black, and Tangel, 2002). This program is designed to help children develop phonemic awareness through activities with alphabet picture cards and jingles, sound categorization, Say-It-and-Move-It (see Figure 6.1) and Elkonin boxes (see Figure 6.2). The beginning activities are auditory, where children segment sounds without using letters. I also chose

Figure 6.1 Say-It-and-Move-It

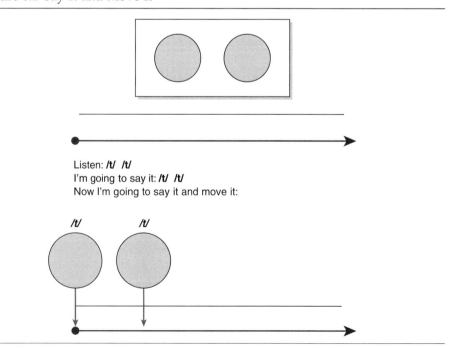

SOURCE: Blachman, B., Ball, E., Black, R., & Tangel, D. (2002). *Road to the Code: A Phonological Awareness Program for Young Children.* Baltimore, MD: Brookes.

Figure 6.2 Elkonin Boxes

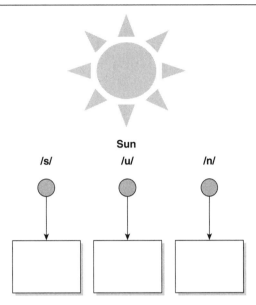

SOURCE: Elkonin, D. B. (1973). U.S.S.R. In J. Downing (Ed.), *Comparative Reading*. New York: MacMillan, pp. 551–580.

to use *Word Building* (Beck, 1999) to help the students with decoding. In *Word Building*, the teacher uses letter cards or tiles and has students build a word, read it, change one letter, and read the resulting word [see Figure 6.3]. The children also read these words and high-frequency sight words in silly sentences to practice using new skills in context."

Group 2: "Because students in Group 2 met the middle-of-first-grade benchmarks and were reading consistently at grade level, I felt this group would benefit from the new word study program, *Phonics Lessons: Letters, Words, and How They Work: Grade 1* (Fountas & Pinnell, 2002). I needed to figure out how to use the program anyway, and this group would be able to deal with less structure."

Group 3: "These students seemed to have a firm grasp of phoneme segmentation and oral reading, but when I looked carefully at their Nonsense Word Fluency task of the DIBELS, several students had some confusion with long- and short-vowel sounds. I set out to learn more about their orthographic [written] knowledge. I gave them the *Elementary Spelling Inventory 1* from the *Words Their Way* program (Bear, Invernizzi, Templeton, & Johnston, 2003). Students all fell into the within-word pattern spelling stage, which means that they know short vowels and consonant-vowel-consonant (CVC) patterns and are ready to begin exploring consonant blends and digraphs and common long-vowel patterns. I chose to use the *Words Their Way* program, where we would sort words and pictures of words containing various short- and long-vowel patterns."

Figure 6.3 Word Building

Students' letters	a	d	n	s	t
Teacher: Bring down the a and put it first. Bring down the n and put it next. Bring down the t and put it last. What word did you build?	a a a	 n n	 t		
Put back the t.	a	n			
Bring down the d. What's the new word?	a	n	d		

Silly Sentence: "Can an ant sit in sand?"

Each lesson of word building held the same structure:

Model

- Demonstrate building a word with magnetic letters (e.g., *cat*)
- Tell students the word; have students repeat ("This word is *cat*. What word is it?")
- Explain that you can change one letter to make a new word
- Model: ("I'm going to take off the 'c' and replace it with a 'b.' I made a new word, *bat*. What word?")
- Have students read the new word

Build/Read

- Give students a set of letters needed to build target words
- Tell students what letters to bring down ("Bring down the 'c' and put it first; bring down the 'a' and put it next; bring down the 't.'")
- Ask students to read word built
- Lead them through building new words by asking them to change one letter at a time ("Take off the 'c' and bring down the 'b' instead."); read each new word
- List the words built
- Have students read the list of words

Silly Sentences

- Write "Silly Sentences" (sentence strips, transparency, board)
- Have students read
- Give students copies to illustrate
- Have students put sentences into personal word building books

Table 6.1 Jenn's Schedule

Time	What was Jenn doing?	What were other students doing?
Beginning of the Day	Introducing picture or word sort concepts from *Words Their Way* to <u>Group 3</u>, giving directions for their independent word study work later in the morning	Morning meeting (calendar, morning message, etc.) **with student teacher**
Independent Reading Time	Teaching word study to <u>Group 1</u> using *Road to the Code* and *Word Building* (These students often struggled to read for the thirty-minute independent reading time, so Jenn uses this as instructional time.)	Independent reading (thirty minutes); students practice reading their book collections aloud with reading phones or silently and complete response journals (This was an established routine, so students knew what was expected.)
Guided Reading Time	Providing an initial mini-lesson on concept to <u>Group 2</u> (They would then do practice activities in the literacy center.)	Group Work <u>Group 1</u>: Guided reading **with reading specialist** <u>Group 3</u>: Word sorts independently (based on Jenn's instructions earlier in the morning)

Coordinating Groups

Jenn planned to provide instruction for each group at least three times a week for a minimum of fifteen minutes. Doing this in a first-grade classroom requires organization. Jenn's time schedule is in Table 6.1. She also had some classroom organization that helped. All students had a small collection of appropriate books that she had already chosen. The classroom routine was one where the students took these books out and read whenever they finished with work or had extra time. Jenn also planned the differentiated word study instruction at times that she had extra help in the classroom.

Classroom Research Tip #3:
Use HELP if you have it.

Table 6.2 Group 1 Instruction

Activity	Description
Road to the Code 1. Say-It-and-Move-It (Figure 6.1)	• Give students a "say-it-and-move-it" mat/paper and chips/markers to put in the rectangle (amount depends on lesson) • Say a single phoneme (e.g., /t/) or phonemes (e.g., /i/ /i/) • Have student repeat the phoneme(s), then repeat each phoneme while simultaneously sliding one chip/marker to the bold line (As the program progresses, the number of sounds/markers increases, then letters replace markers to represent the phonemes.)
2. Sound Categorization	• Give students four picture cards (e.g., dog, duck, car, dollar) • Have students find the picture that does not belong (doesn't rhyme or doesn't contain the same initial sound); ask why students chose that picture
3. Letter Sounds	• Introduce letters, picture, sounds, and jingle • Have students practice saying letter sound, picture, and jingle (e.g., "M, monkey, /m/." Clap: "Mike the marvelous monkey.")
4. Fish and Bingo	• Play sound Bingo or Fish to practice sounds
5. Elkonin cards (Figure 6.2)	• Give students Elkonin cards with a picture on top and boxes representing the corresponding number of sounds at the bottom • Have students say the word slowly, sliding a marker into each box for each sound in the word

Step 5: Jenn Implements Her Plan and Collects Data.

Implementing the Plan

Now that Jenn had her plans in place, she followed her plans for each group. Group 1 instruction followed a predictable sequence. Their plan is in Table 6.2.

Jenn did not have a consistent structure for Group 2; it depended on the concept being taught. She used a variety of mini-lessons with corresponding literacy center activities from the *Phonics Lessons* (Fountas & Pinnell, 2002) program. *Phonics Lessons* consists of instruction and activities in nine word study categories. Because Group 2 students had established some of these concepts, Jenn focused on areas of need including high-frequency words, spelling patterns, word structure, word-solving actions, and word meaning.

Table 6.3 Group 3 Instruction

Activity: Words Their Way	Description
Cutting	Give students a sheet of twenty pictures and/or words with three letters or picture headers representing the sounds for sorting (e.g., *ee feet, e bed, oddball*); have students cut the pictures apart and place the headings at the top of their tables
Introducing Sound and Pattern	Introduce the sounds and patterns for sorting to make sure the students are clear
Sorting	Have students sort the pictures and words according to the sound or pattern headers
Pasting	Have students paste their sorts into their word study notebooks
Checking	Check students' word study notebooks
Meeting	If needed, meet with students who did not grasp the sort
Assessment	Give brief spelling assessment after finishing each particular pattern (e.g., vowel-consonant-e)

Jenn followed a predictable structure for the *Words Their Way* (Bear et al., 2003) lessons used for Group 3 instruction. Table 6.3 shows Jenn's typical instructional sequence for this group.

Collecting the Data

Jenn administered the same DIBELS subtests to all students again during the first week of April and scored these according to the end-of-first-grade benchmarks.

Step 6: Jenn Analyzes the Data.

For Jenn, analyzing the data was very straightforward. She simply graphed the students' scores on each subtest of the DIBELS and then looked at these scores by groups (see Figures 6.4, 6.5, and 6.6). Students in Group 1, who were below all benchmarks initially, made tremendous progress on average. Students in Group 2, who initially met all middle-of-first-grade benchmarks, now met all end-of-first-grade benchmarks. Students in Group 3, who initially met all of the end-of first-grade benchmarks for all three subtests, continued to do so.

Step 7: Jenn Reflects on the Data and What It Means.

Jenn learned a lot about her students and her instruction from this project. She discusses some of her insights: "All three groups made gains in all

Figure 6.4 Students' Scores, by Group, on the DIBELS Phoneme Segmentation Task Pre- and Post-Instruction (January and April). For this task, 37 or more correct indicates that students' phoneme segmentation is "established."

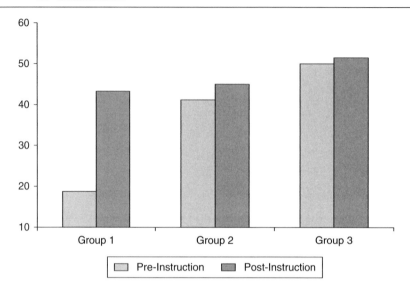

Figure 6.5 Students' Scores, by Group, on the DIBELS Nonsense Word Fluency Task Pre- and Post-Instruction (January and April). For this task, 50 or more correct indicates that students' decoding skills are "established."

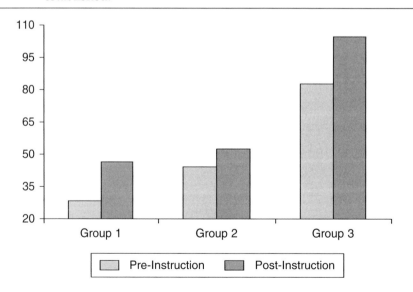

Figure 6.6 Students' Scores, by Group, on the DIBELS Oral Reading Fluency Task Pre- and Post-Instruction (January and April). For this task, students are considered at "low risk" if they can read 40 or more words per minute.

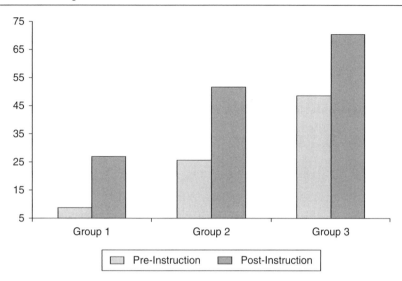

areas assessed; however, it was in varying amounts. Group 1 made the largest gains in phoneme segmentation, moving from "at-risk" to "established." The *Road to the Code* program, which I had not previously used, is designed specifically to address segmentation. Through activities such as "Say-It-and-Move-It," and Elkonin cards, the students practiced listening for and segmenting sounds in words. These students also made considerable gains in nonsense word reading and oral reading fluency. *Word Building*, another program I had not used before, is designed specifically to work on decoding. This suggests to me that differentiating instruction—selecting and providing two programs (that I typically would not have provided) based on my students' needs—made a significant difference for this group of struggling students. I only wonder whether these students would have made even more progress if I had begun differentiating earlier in the year.

"My Group 2 and Group 3 students, the on- and above-grade level students, made little gain in phonemic segmentation, but didn't need to work on this skill, and weren't provided instruction in it. They made adequate gains in decoding and oral reading fluency, using two different programs designed for whole-class instruction. This suggests to me that students who already have the skills will continue to make gains given good whole-class instruction. I can't be sure this is due to differentiated instruction—in other words, I don't know whether these groups would have made these gains without using the word study activities from *Words Their Way* or the *Phonics Lessons*."

Step 8: Jenn Thinks About the Future.

Given the success of differentiating the word study portion of her instruction, Jenn is convinced that she needs to differentiate other areas of instruction as well. She comments on what she calls *The Bottom Line:* "Differentiated word study has been most important to students performing below grade level. Although some may still need intervention in some areas, they made gains in areas that the whole-class program I was asked to use did not address consistently and at a point in the year where most first-grade programs assume students already have basic skills such as phonemic awareness. This suggests to me that in a whole-class design, it is almost guaranteed that there will be children left behind, which is unacceptable."

Jenn's project required a great deal of planning and organization to accomplish. I asked Jenn to comment on how others might create this kind of instruction in their classrooms. Here is her advice: "When I think about how other teachers might design an effective differentiated word study program for their classroom, I'm still not sure that I have determined a clear way to achieve this. I had support in my classroom—thirty minutes a day from a literacy teacher, thirty minutes from the literacy assistant, and, during the time I implemented this research, a very competent student teacher. This is how I was able to keep my classroom functioning while I worked intensely with each group of students, particularly when learning these new techniques for instructing word study groups became more time consuming than I anticipated. I know that others might not be as fortunate. Additionally, because I was pursuing advanced education in reading, I learned about three of the programs I used in this research. Otherwise, I would not have known they existed. I know that other teachers try to supplement instruction with additional materials, but have little time and may not know how to search for the best researched-based programs. Most programs published claim to be systematic and sequential, but that doesn't mean that they are.

"So, how could other teachers design an effective differentiated word study program? Teachers would need a variety of current research-based programs available to them, and professional development to learn how to assess their students, match programs to students, and implement these programs. The responsibility for this would lie with school administrators, reading specialists, and curriculum coordinators. But I have begun to share what I did and work with teachers to find creative ways to use our human resources to accomplish it. Now many more teachers are differentiating their instruction."

WRAP UP

Jenn's project has shown us a lot about the nitty-gritty of dealing with logistics. Jenn carefully planned how to get the materials she wanted and needed, how to coordinate her schedule so that she had help when she needed it, and how to share with others what she wanted and needed them to do. Although this was a lot of work, her pre-planning paid off in the long run. She was able to juggle three different groups of first graders using three different programs and evaluate the students and the programs at the same time.

Jenn's project has also shown us that differentiating instruction can and does make a difference in students' learning. A one-size-fits-all model is not going to meet the needs of all students. By using two new programs specifically targeted toward her students' needs, she significantly raised their skills in these areas. We cannot say that students would not have made progress with the other programs, but given that Jenn began her project in January, we can say that they had not, as of yet, gained these skills. On the other hand, Jenn's project also confirmed what she learned from her inquiry: The programs did not seem to matter for the students who were on or above grade level. As long as instruction was sequential and structured, students made progress.

HOW DOES JENN'S PROJECT RELATE TO YOU?

You have now read two pieces of research conducted in Grade 1. Keep in mind that I chose to include these projects for their applicability to any grade. Differentiating instruction is not merely a "first-grade thing." It applies to any subject in any grade. If we want to be successful at differentiating instruction, we need to plan it, or it will surely become overwhelming. Differentiating means assessing where students are, grouping them to target specific areas of instruction, choosing instruction targeted to needs, and monitoring progress. We all benefit from trying this kind of practice.

YOU TRY IT

Your task in this chapter will serve two purposes: first, to continue your planning for your own research, and second, to help you determine whether you need to think about differentiating your instruction. Using the data chart you created for your task from Chapter 5, review the data to answer these questions.

- Do all students have the same knowledge in the area you assessed?
- If not, do there appear to be patterns in your data (for example, students who have difficulty with a specific skill)?

Try to group your students according to their strengths and needs.

Tying Research to Practice

In this section we move up the grades to look at how teachers translate research into practice in primary, intermediate, middle, and high school classrooms. Although you will read about projects at specific grade levels, you can use these teachers' topics and ideas in your own classroom at your own grade level by thinking about the suggestions in the section of each chapter titled, "How Does This Apply to You?"

7

"Mr. [Smith] Just Said Rambunctious!"

Learning and Loving Vocabulary

Classroom Research Spotlight
Step 2: Inquire
Step 8: Plan

Literacy Spotlight
Vocabulary Teaching and Learning

While I was visiting Jayne's classroom, a student virtually skidded into the room shouting, "Mrs. Ward, Mr. [Smith] just said *rambunctious*!" "Why did he say that?" Jayne asked. "Because we were all slamming our lockers!" This chapter explains how this second-grade teacher helped her students become users and observers of wonderful words.

I have chosen to highlight both Step 2 (Inquire) and Step 8 (Plan) in this chapter. Jayne's vocabulary project is actually a continuation of a project she had begun the previous year. Like Maureen in Chapter 4, Jayne had been working on developing her discussion techniques using Beck & McKeown's (2001) *Text Talk* model. When Jayne analyzed her transcripts, she could see her students were engaged and, among them, could create meaning from sophisticated text. She could also see that she was progressing as a discussion facilitator, meeting her goals of really analyzing the text to identify places to stop and discuss, creating productive queries, and allowing the students to do most of the talking. However, analyzing her discussion transcripts also showed Jayne how vocabulary was often a major stumbling block to students creating full meaning from the text. Jayne gave significant thought to the issue of vocabulary. What's going on with vocabulary? Why is it such a stumbling block? This analysis and reflection (Steps 6 and 7) led to Jayne's next action plan (Step 8)—identify a new question and begin the cycle again. We pick up Jayne's project at this point in time.

JAYNE'S RESEARCH

Context for Jayne's Project.

Jayne teaches nineteen second-grade students in a small, K–2, White, middle-class, suburban school. Because it is a primary school, no state assessments are administered, so there is no data regarding school performance classification. Jayne was in a unique position; she shared her teaching position with another teacher, each of them teaching two and a half days per week. Jayne began implementing this part of her research in February.

Step 1: Jayne Notices Issues in Her Research.

Jayne's noticing began in Step 6 (Analyze) of her previous research using *Text Talk*. She was intrigued by how vocabulary could make or break students' understanding of text.

Step 2: Jayne Inquires Into Vocabulary.

When Jayne turned to research on vocabulary, she encountered many "a-ha" moments.

Vocabulary Is VERY Related to Comprehension!

For decades, the relationship between comprehension and vocabulary has been a "given" in the field of reading. Many researchers suggest that the achievement gap in reading, particularly in comprehension, between socioeconomic groups is predominantly related to a "language gap" (Hirsch, 2001), or a significant gap between students with enriched versus limited vocabulary (Biemiller, 2001; Chall, Jacobs, & Baldwin, 1991; Moats, 2001a; Snow, Barnes, Chandler, Goodman, & Hemphill, 1991). The "language gap" is more than simply a dearth of vocabulary knowledge; it is a cycle that is fed (or not fed) by vocabulary. In an often-cited work, Stanovich (1986) talked about a reciprocal relationship between vocabulary and reading; what he termed "Matthew Effects" (based on a phrase from the book of Matthew, "He who hath shall have in abundance; he who hath not shall lose even that which he hath.") Students with strong vocabulary are more likely to read widely, which, in turn, fosters incidental vocabulary learning, which, in turn, helps students comprehend texts of increasing difficulty; students with limited vocabulary tend not to read widely, which limits vocabulary growth, making reading less and less likely, and understanding less and less easy. In this way, students who enter school with limited vocabulary are already at a disadvantage compared to their vocabulary-rich peers.

Children Learn Vocabulary in Lots of Ways!

All children learn vocabulary from sources outside of school and reading. In fact, a great deal of vocabulary growth occurs before a child even enters school and learns to read. The average child enters first grade knowing approximately 6,000 words! Once children enter school, they learn anywhere from 1,000 to 3,000 words per year (Goulden, Nation, & Read, 1990; Nagy, 1998). With a moderate to high rate of learning, by the end of high school our average student now knows 25,000 to 45,000 words! Impressive, yet daunting! How do students learn this many words?

One way students learn words is through reading. "Good" readers in Grades 3–9 read approximately one million words per year (Nagy & Anderson, 1984). This gives the average student lots of opportunities to encounter and learn novel words. Out of 100 unfamiliar words, students learn about five to fifteen through context (Nagy, Herman, & Anderson, 1985)—that is, if a student reads widely enough to encounter lots of new words and if a student has the skills to gain a word's meaning from context (Beck, McKeown, & Kucan, 2002). In addition, students learn words through oral language, talking, and listening to others.

If children are learning new words through reading and listening, why should we teach vocabulary? Many of our struggling readers do not read widely (Juel, 1988). A "good" reader reads more than 200 times more words than a "struggling" reader (Anderson, Wilson, & Fielding, 1988), which means that struggling readers are not encountering lots of new words when reading, so they are not enriching their vocabularies. This is of particular concern because this vocabulary, or language, gap is hard to close (Biemiller, 1999; Hart & Risley, 1995). We DO need to worry about vocabulary instruction.

TEACHING Vocabulary Makes a Difference!

Jayne found that emphasizing vocabulary instruction in the classroom can and does make a difference in comprehension (Beck, Perfetti, & McKeown, 1982; Stahl & Fairbanks, 1986) and in vocabulary acquisition (Stahl & Fairbanks, 1986). Teachers can promote vocabulary through *indirect* instruction—reading aloud to students (Dickinson & Smith, 1994; Elley, 1988), using repeated read alouds (Senachal & Cornell, 1993), and encouraging wide and varied reading (Robbins & Ehri, 1994). There are also many ways to provide *direct* vocabulary instruction—instruction where the teacher tells students definitions or other characteristics of words, or teaches students how to gain word meaning through context. Some examples include rich instruction (Beck, McKeown, & Kucan, 2002), pre-teaching vocabulary (Brett, Rothlein, & Hurley, 1996), the keyword method (Levin, McCormick, Miller, & Berry, 1984), and teaching students to use context (Kolich, 1991). The most optimal methods provide repeated exposure to words across multiple contexts. However, Jayne learned an important take-home message from vocabulary instruction research: *Any instruction is better than no instruction for vocabulary learning* (National Reading Panel, 2000). We DO need to teach vocabulary.

Jayne also learned that vocabulary learning is not all-or-nothing, but rather a continuum progressing from no knowledge (never seen or heard the word) to recognition (heard or seen the word before) to narrow context-bound knowledge (the word has something to do with . . .), to rich decontextualized knowledge (the word can be defined and used in multiple contexts) (Dale, 1965). This developmental view, and the research on effective vocabulary teaching, showed Jayne that it is important to expose students to many words and, through instruction, help students move specific words along the learning continuum.

Step 3: Jayne Develops Specific Questions.

Jayne decided that she wanted to try rich vocabulary instruction to see how she could enhance students' word knowledge. She wanted to know two things.

Teacher-as-Learner Question
How do I implement rich vocabulary instruction?

Student Learning Questions
If I implement rich instruction, will students learn vocabulary?
How will they move up the vocabulary-learning continuum?

Step 4: Jayne Plans Her Instruction and Data Collection.

Because Jayne had success with the *Text Talk* read-aloud model, she decided to incorporate vocabulary instruction based on the read alouds, as recommended in *Text Talk* (Beck & McKeown, 2001). Jayne felt she had to have everything in place before she began so she could concentrate on instruction. She carefully planned what she would do.

Planning Instruction

Choosing Texts and Words

Jayne tailored her vocabulary instruction to her read-aloud program and modeled it after the recommendations from the book, *Bringing Words to Life* (Beck, McKeown, & Kucan, 2002). In the book, Beck et al. emphasize choosing Tier 2 words. In contrast to Tier 1 words (words that are so well known they need no instruction) and Tier 3 words (words that are best studied within a content area), Tier 2 words are those for which students have the concept but not the label. These are words that can be used across multiple contexts and can be worked with in multiple ways—words such as *marvelous, astonish,* and *rambunctious.*

Classroom Research Tip #4:
Don't reinvent the wheel.
If something already exists, use it.

Because Jayne was trying to assimilate a new instructional technique while continuing to run her classroom, she drew her choice of books and words from *Bringing Words to Life,* which provides lists of grade-appropriate read alouds and corresponding Tier 2 words. Jayne decided that in the span of her research she would read five books and engage students in instruction with the related vocabulary. Table 7.1 shows the books and vocabulary Jayne selected.

Table 7.1 Jayne's Chosen Texts and Vocabulary From Each

Week Introduced	Text	Vocabulary
Week 1	*Metropolitan Cow* By Tim Egan	fortunate, dignified, rambunctious
Week 2	*Eat Your Vegetables* By James Marshall	prefer, ferocious, budge
Week 3	*Little House* By Virginia Lee Burton	notice, glance, shabby
Week 4	*Livingstone Mouse* By Pamela Duncan Edwards	murmur, argumentative, throbbed
Week 5	*Patchwork Quilt* By Valerie Flournoy	masterpiece, miserable, dread

Jayne also wanted to find a way to kick-start her instruction by whetting students' interest in the power of words. She chose to read *Donovan's Word Jar* (DeGross, 1994), where the main character, Donovan, collects interesting words.

Preparing Materials

Once Jayne had chosen books and words, she needed to plan her instruction and prepare her materials. Here is what she did.

- Created a *Wonderful Words* bulletin board on which she posted a copy of the cover of each read-aloud book. She would use the bulletin board to post the vocabulary words she introduced and to tally instances of students reporting they had heard the word used by others (based on the Word Wizard idea in *Bringing Words to Life*).
- Created a *Wonderful Words* journal for each student for them to record their words, student-friendly definitions, illustrations, and sentence-completion activities.
- Gathered two *Wonderful Words* jars to expand the theme of *Donovan's Word Jar*, to place words introduced as part of the instruction in one and other words that students found interesting and wanted to share in the other.

Planning Logistics

Enlisting help (Remember Tip #3: Use help if you have it!)

Jayne knew that her project would be more successful if she created lots of opportunities for students to use the words outside of her classroom. To encourage this, Jayne wrote a letter to her colleagues explaining her project and asking for their support in using the target words. She attached a list of the chosen words and the dates they would be introduced, along with some ideas of how others might incorporate the words into their talk with the students.

Coordinating Instruction

To ensure consistency with her job-share partner, Jayne developed read-aloud and vocabulary protocols for each book. Jayne prepared scripts for the read-aloud instruction. She decided where she wanted to stop reading to help students build meaning. She then inserted into the text Post-it notes containing queries she wanted to pose, follow-up queries to responses she felt students might give, and simple explanations of the target vocabulary words so students could understand the text. For the vocabulary instruction, Jayne designed a five-day cycle for each set of words. The general protocol for the story reading and vocabulary work is shown in Table 7.2. An example of the activities for one story, "Eat Your Vegetables," from *Rats on the Roof* (Marshall, 1997) is provided in Table 7.3.

Planning Data Collection

Jayne was interested in knowing whether her instruction mattered to students' learning, which was probably the most difficult aspect of her planning.

Table 7.2 Jayne's Read Aloud and Vocabulary Weekly Schedule

Day	Activity
Day 1 Wednesday	• Read aloud incorporating discussion based on *Text Talk* model • State the meaning of the selected vocabulary words when they arise in the text ("budge means to move something the tiniest bit") • Introduce vocabulary words after reading
Day 2 Thursday	• Review the student-friendly definitions of the selected vocabulary, recording them on a transparency • Have students say how they can use the word in a different context ("I can't budge my sister when she is watching TV.") • Have students write the words and their meanings in their *Wonderful Words* journal • Have students illustrate one selected word in their journal
Day 3 Friday	• On chart paper, write sentence starters containing the selected vocabulary; discuss possible endings to the sentences • Have the students decide on one ending for the sentence • Write the ending on the chart • Have students write the sentences in their *Wonderful Words* journal
Day 4 Monday	• Engage students in the making choices activity • Have students illustrate another selected word
Day 5 Tuesday	• Build connections among the words by presenting situations using all words • Have students try to connect all words • Have students illustrate the final word

Jayne went back to the research she read in Step 2 to find out how those studies measured students' vocabulary knowledge. The National Reading Panel (2000) recommends that the best vocabulary assessments are those that are closely tied to the curriculum. This meant Jayne had to create her own assessment, tied to the words she would teach. She created two measures: one to assess students' ability to generate meanings by writing down what the words meant, and one multiple choice task where students chose a synonym for a given word out of four possible choices. Jayne also wanted to find out how much students noticed the words being used outside of the classroom. She planned to record a tally mark beneath the appropriate word on the *Wonderful Words* bulletin board each time children reported they heard the word outside of class and in what context.

Step 5: Jayne Implements Her Plan and Collects Data.

With the detail Jayne paid to planning, implementing the project was easy. She introduced *Donovan's Word Jar* (DeGross, 1994), discussing with the students the importance and power of words and how they all were about to undertake their own collection of words as they read interesting and wonderful stories. She introduced the *Wonderful Words* journals, bulletin board, and jars. Jayne began her five-day cycle for each book and group of words on a Wednesday and completed it on a Tuesday, which

Table 7.3 Jayne's Vocabulary Activities for Week 2, "Eat Your Vegetables," From *Rats on the Roof* (Marshall, 1997)

Day	Activity/Example
Wednesday Introduce Vocabulary	• Contextualize how the word was used in the story. • Provide a student-friendly definition. • Ask students to say the word. • Provide an example of how to use the word outside the story. • Have student provide examples. • Have students repeat the word.
Thursday Review	• Review: What are the words we've been talking about? (*prefer, ferocious, budge*). We said that *prefer* means to choose one thing over another. I would say that for dessert, I *prefer* ice cream rather than cake. • Have students give examples of how they might use each word: How can you use *prefer*? Make sure you use the word *prefer* when you give your example. • Have students copy the words and their meanings into their journals: Turn to a new page in your journal. Write the word *prefer* at the top. Then write our definition of *prefer*: to choose one thing over another. (Repeat with all words.) • Draw a picture of *prefer* on its page of your journals.
Friday Sentence Completion	Write sentence starters on transparency: • I *prefer* the beach to a pool because . . . • The class would not *budge* from their seats when . . . • The zookeeper said the lion was *ferocious* because . . . Let's read this sentence, "I prefer the beach to a pool because . . ." how can we end that sentence? Who has an idea? (Allow children to discuss. Choose one ending for each word and write on transparency.) Copy these examples into your journals on the page for each word.

Day	Activity/Example

Monday
 	
Making
Choices
	Say *budge* if any of these would be difficult to move. If not, don't say anything.
	
	  • a large boulder • a sleeping mule
	  • a pencil • a marble
	  • a tree stump • your mom's decision
	
	I'll say some things. If anything sounds *ferocious,* say "ferocious"; if not, don't say anything
	
	  • a puppy • a baby
	  • a T-Rex • a hungry tiger
	  • a 120-degree room • your teacher
	
	Raise one finger if you *prefer* choice #1, or two fingers if you prefer choice #2:
	
	• Do you *prefer* pizza with cheese or pizza with pepperoni?
	• Do you *prefer* pasta with butter or pasta with sauce?
	• Do you *prefer* riding a bike or riding a scooter?
	• Do you *prefer* going to the movies or going to the library?
	
	Draw a picture of *ferocious* on its page of your journal.

Tuesday Relate the Words	Would you *prefer* to *budge* a sleeping lamb or a *ferocious* lion? Why? (Beck et al., 2002, p. 58) Would you try to *budge* a ferocious panther? Why? Would you try to *budge* your dog? Why? Illustrate the word *budge* on its page of your journal.

ensured that Jayne was the one to conduct the discussion of each story and introduce the target vocabulary. Each vocabulary lesson lasted approximately twenty minutes. The *Text Talk* (story reading) on Day 1 was an additional thirty minutes.

Once Jayne introduced the vocabulary project, she told her students that she wanted to see what they knew about words before they began. She then read aloud each of the fifteen target words and asked the students to write down what the words meant or anything they knew about the words. She then read aloud the multiple-choice assessment items and asked the students to circle the word that most closely matched each target word. She gave students these same assessments after she completed the five books.

On the *Wonderful Words* board, Jayne recorded a tally mark next to a particular word whenever students noted staff members, Jayne, or others using the word. Students needed to be able to state how they heard or saw (read) the particular word being used. When a word earned ten tally marks, students earned a small reward.

Step 6: Jayne Analyzes the Data.

For the multiple-choice task, Jayne calculated the number of correct responses for each student and the number of students who chose the correct synonym for each word (giving her student and word data). She then compared the average (mean) scores for pre- and post-instruction using a simple statistical test (T-test).

Working with another teacher, who was also researching vocabulary (Classroom Research Tip #3: Use help if you have it!), Jayne created a four-point rubric based on the word knowledge continuum (Dale, 1965) discussed earlier (see Table 7.4).

Jayne charted the results of the word tallies (see Figure 7.1), multiple-choice task (see Figures 7.2 and 7.3), and developmental continuum (see Figure 7.4). The data show that her students did gain knowledge of the words taught. Students could choose a correct synonym out of four choices on the multiple-choice task. [Out of fifteen total words, students could choose the correct answer for an average of 7.6 words at the beginning of the project and fourteen words at the end (p = <.05)]. In general, students moved up the developmental continuum on all words. Most students (twelve out of fourteen) had little to no knowledge of the words before the instruction began, yet many could define words in a specific situation at the end (see Figure 7.4).

Step 7: Jayne Reflects on the Data and What It Means.

The tally and developmental continuum data showed that students heard, observed, and defined the words introduced through the last two books (*murmur, argumentative, throbbed, masterpiece, miserable, dread*) less often than the words introduced earlier. She assumed this was due to less opportunity for instruction and exposure (less time). However, Jayne also noted some words introduced earlier that students did not report hearing (for example, *shabby* and *ferocious*). Cross-checking her other data, Jayne noted that this was not because students did not know these words. In fact, the word *shabby* was one of the least well defined at the beginning and the most well defined at the end. Something else was going on. Looking over these data, Jayne noticed that some of the words heard less often had a negative meaning. Perhaps this makes them harder for others to use? For example, how would an adult use the word *shabby* (meaning disheveled) around a child in a way that would not be construed as negative? Or perhaps some words just had more appeal to these second graders and the greater school community. Words such as *rambunctious* and *notice* definitely were heard more and moved farther

Table 7.4 Examples of Students' Written Definitions Fitting Each Point on the
Word Knowledge Development Rubric (Before Instruction)

Word	Rubric Score/Definition			
	1 Doesn't know	2 Has seen or heard before	3 Can relate to situation	4 Can define
Fortunate	No response [left blank] "?" "I bont no" [I don't know] "You thik you know a lot of stoff"	"mene" [money] "rich" "menes speshle" [means special] "you have a lot of mone"	"You have effet" [you have everything] "when you make a forchen"	None
Dignified	No response [left blank] "?" "I dont' no" "got cote" [got caught] "it is big"	"Yur smarte" [you're smart]	None	None
Rambunctious	No response [left blank] "?" "siging" [singing] "it mens you thingking" [It means you're thinking] "you have a lot of friends"	"your being playfull" "your ecsited" [you're excited]	"when you go crozei" [crazy] "you are crase [crazy] and silly" "wieled" [wild]	None

along the continuum. This led to another "a-ha" moment for Jayne:
Choosing words is more important than she thought.

In addition to learning about words, Jayne learned lessons about classroom research and lessons about vocabulary teaching and learning. She
talks about each of these in turn: "I can use action research! I can monitor
students' learning to help inform my instructional practices. Rather than
think an instructional program is working, collecting data in a systematic

Figure 7.1 Results of Jayne's Tally Chart Showing How Many Times Students Reported they Heard the Words Used by Others. Words are listed in order of the week in which they were introduced (i.e., *fortunate, dignified,* and *rambunctious* were introduced in Week 1; whereas *masterpiece, miserable,* and *dread* were introduced in Week 5), explaining some of the difference in usage.

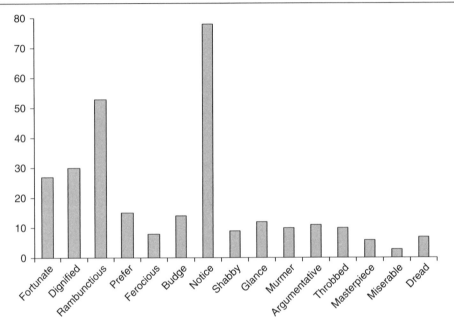

Figure 7.2 The Average Number of Words Jayne's Students Correctly Identified on the Multiple-Choice Task Before and After the Instruction. There were fifteen words taught.

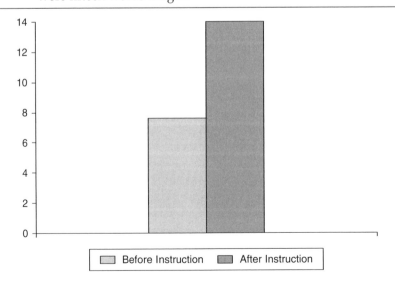

Figure 7.3 Students' Scores on the Pre- and Post-Instruction Multiple-Choice
Task. The bars represent the number of students who correctly
identified the meaning of each word out of four possible choices.

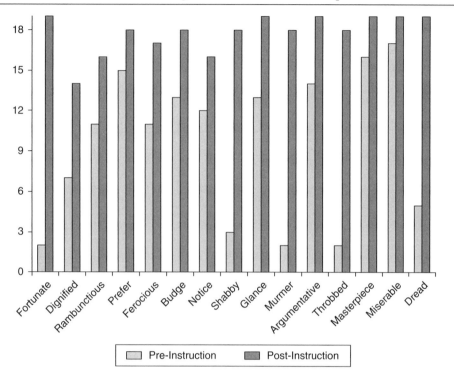

Figure 7.4 The Average Number of Students Scoring at Each Point on
the Vocabulary Development Rubric Across Words Before and
After Instruction

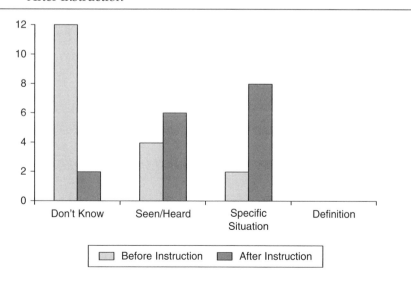

way shows me the instruction is working. Doing something that works and showing others gets them excited to follow!

"I can build thoughtful vocabulary instruction into an already crowded schedule. Rich vocabulary instruction is motivating and important to my students and has helped my students learn words and love language!"

Jayne recognized that her understanding of her students' vocabulary learning was based on her own assessment of it. She gave thoughtful consideration to this. With the open-ended definition assessment, Jayne was trying to assess students' independent knowledge of words. However, some students may not have been able to spell what they wanted to say, or simply became tired and gave up without fully describing their knowledge. Jayne felt that if she had dictated the words and scribed students' answers, although more time-consuming, she would have increased the likelihood that she could trust students' responses were the best they could do. Jayne also felt she should have gotten a handle on how *students* used the target words, in addition to how they heard others use them. This was her original intent, but she had not anticipated students' enthusiasm. They were calling out, talking about words during other subjects, etc. It just became too much to keep track of. If she were to do a project like this again, she would better anticipate and plan how to capture this data.

Step 8: Jayne Creates an Action Plan.

One of the unforeseen outcomes of Jayne's study was that her colleagues were intrigued by students' motivation and interest in the words they were learning and in other words that they had heard, and wanted to learn more about what Jayne was doing. Because Jayne had planned so well, she was able to give her lessons to her colleagues. Now other teachers are teaching wonderful words. They all create and share instructional scripts across classrooms, making planning much easier. Even other adults in the school got involved in this project. The physical education teacher made it a point to pay attention to his word choices—students *preferred* one game over another, *noticed* how a game was played, kept their voices to a *murmur*, and were certainly not *argumentative* about rules. Other adults in the school carefully used words as well. Lastly, Jayne was amazed at the students' enthusiasm for this project. They learned to love words! They found new words daily. When Jayne read aloud, they pointed out when an author used a wonderful word (or in some cases noted a wonderful word the author *could have* used instead of the word the author did use), they chose better words in their writing, and they became more mature language users.

WRAP UP

Jayne's project showcases the inquiry and planning involved in classroom research. Jayne had to plan not only for herself, but for her job-share partner. (Remember Classroom Research Tip #1: You can conduct classroom research even when you're not there.) Having prepared scripts for her read alouds and vocabulary instruction and having her five-day cycle charted out allowed Jayne's partner to step in and keep the project running during her half of the week. Jayne also used help in a variety of ways. (Classroom Research Tip #3: Use help if you have it!). Her classroom teaching partner was an instrumental part of her research, but seeking help from other adults provided students with additional language models to extend their learning.

Jayne's research also shows us the importance of vocabulary in comprehension, and the power of direct vocabulary instruction. Teaching definitions will only go so far if students do not have the opportunity to use the words and hear them being used outside of the classroom. This idea of rich instruction—teaching and using words in a variety of ways—is a useful tool in vocabulary teaching. Of course, we cannot teach students every word they are ever going to know or need to know. But Jayne's project has helped us see that we do not need to teach every word. We need to choose our words carefully. By targeting words that can be used in multiple ways across multiple contexts, we can increase the likelihood that what we teach will stick, thereby increasing our students' repertoire of mature vocabulary.

HOW DOES JAYNE'S PROJECT RELATE TO YOU?

What Jayne learned about vocabulary applies to everyone in a school setting. We all need to teach words, regardless of what we teach. New words crop up everywhere. For some of us, vocabulary instruction means starting at the beginning with Tier 1 (very common) words. For example, if you teach English Language Learners (ELL), you will most likely need to teach Tier 1, 2, and 3 words. If you teach science, you will be focused on teaching Tier 3 (specialty) words. But if we learned anything from the idea of rich instruction it is that teaching words means using words. We cannot simply give definitions and expect words to instantly move up the vocabulary continuum. We need to provide students with the opportunity to use words in a variety of ways.

YOU TRY IT

You have another classroom research task here to extend the planning you have already done. You also have a task to help you think about vocabulary.

Classroom Research Task.

Continue the planning for your own research but pay particular attention to logistics—what you will need to do to accomplish your instructional goal. Refer back to Table 1.7 and address those logistical concerns.

Literacy Task.

Observe how your students are using vocabulary in and outside of the classroom. Start with the vocabulary connected to the research you are designing. If you do not feel that you need to think about vocabulary within your research, think about the subject area you teach. What vocabulary do you need to teach? Are your words Tier 1, Tier 2, or Tier 3 words? Chart out the words that are important for your students to learn. How will you teach them? How will you get students interested and excited about learning words?

8

Sounding Like Readers

Improving Fluency

Classroom Research Spotlight
Step 7: Reflect
(Cycling Through Steps 6–7)

Literacy Spotlight
Fluency

Richard Allington, former president of the International Reading Association and noted reading researcher, once termed reading fluency the "neglected goal" of reading (Allington, 1983). However, teachers are becoming more aware of the need to help students develop reading fluency, particularly since the National Reading Panel (2000) included fluency as one of the core areas of reading. In this chapter, Ruth Lynn, a third-grade teacher, shares her fluency program. The spotlight for this chapter is on Step 7, Reflect. Ruth Lynn's results appeared puzzling at first. However, she was able to reflect and revisit her analyses to put the pieces together.

RUTH LYNN'S RESEARCH

Context for Ruth Lynn's Project.

Ruth Lynn's third-grade class is in a "high performing" K–4 elementary school in a small, suburban school district. The student population is predominantly White of moderate income. Her school has a large proportion of children from naval families, which results in a high mobility rate.

Step 1: Ruth Lynn Notices What's Going On.

Fluency was something that Ruth Lynn had been thinking about for some time. She explains, "I became interested in fluency for a couple of reasons. First, I was tutoring a fourth-grade boy who struggled in reading. His skills were actually not that bad, but when he put them all together to read connected text, he sounded like a robot. His comprehension was OK, but not great. I felt that his lack of fluency was a part of this comprehension picture. Second, many of the students in my third-grade classroom also had trouble with fluency. They read slowly, word-by-word, in an unexpressive way. I wondered how I could help students develop more fluent reading."

Step 2: Ruth Lynn Inquires Into Fluency.

Ruth Lynn researched what fluency is all about. Here is what she found.

Fluency Is a Small Word for a Big Process

Fluency is often defined as rate (words per minute) and accuracy (percentage of words correctly read) because these are easy to measure. But fluency is more than that. When students read fluently, they also read smoothly with appropriate prosody (phrasing) and expression. Students who are not fluent may read at a slow, halting pace, making frequent mistakes and using poor phrasing and inadequate intonation (Hook & Jones, 2002). However, even expanding fluency to include more than rate and accuracy, we are still talking about reading texts (paragraphs, chapters, books), which means that we miss important things about fluency. Fluency actually involves every process and sub-process of reading (Wolf & Katzir-Cohen, 2001). In other words, in order to read a paragraph, chapter, or book *fluently*, a reader must also be able to identify letters, word patterns, and words quickly and accurately, and equally quickly and accurately access vocabulary meanings. But these skills do not all develop at once.

Fluency Is Developmental

Fluency begins below the word level (letters, sounds, and word parts) and continues to blossom. Fluent readers must develop accuracy (correctness) and automaticity (quickness) with lots of little parts of the reading process—identifying letter sounds, using strategies for accurately decoding new words, and identifying high-frequency words. So, at first, a reader is not fluent. Beginning readers typically read word-by-word, trying to coordinate all that is involved in figuring out the text. In a seminal volume on reading development, Jeanne Chall (1983) called this being "glued to print." However, as children gain more experience with letters and words, they begin to identify them automatically, without consciously thinking about them. Then, as they begin to automatize letters, words, and strategies, they begin to move from word-by-word reading to grouping words together meaningfully and more quickly. Chall (1983) called this becoming "unglued from print," and marked this as one of the hallmarks of reading.

Fluency Is Important to Comprehension

Fluent reading helps students understand and remember more of what they read and gain vocabulary knowledge. If readers cannot get words off the page automatically, they must consciously pay attention to the print. Yet, readers can only concentrate on so many things at once. If they are spending too much attention and concentration on getting words off the page, they will have little left over for understanding the text (Laberge & Samuels, 1974).

Making room in the brain for more important thinking processes is one way that fluency helps comprehension. Another is when readers "chunk" text into particular phrases. Certain words (e.g., prepositions, conjunctions) signal how a text should be chunked (consider this phrasing: "He / put his / hat on, / the table." versus this: "He / put his hat / on the table."), as does punctuation. If readers do not pay attention to these text signals, they may not chunk the text appropriately, which will interfere with comprehension.

It Is Possible to Improve Fluency Through Instruction

Students need models of fluent reading. Read aloud is perfect for this, at any grade. (High school students will better understand and read Shakespeare if they hear what the language should sound like.) Teachers reading aloud model expressive reading, reading dialogue, phrasing, and intonation. In addition to reading aloud, teachers should help students develop fluency all along its developmental path, such as speed games at the letter and word level, phrase reading, phrase cued text, and practice with whole texts. Rasinski (2003) describes many of these strategies in his book, *The Fluent Reader*.

A well-researched technique at the connected text level is guided repeated oral reading (known as "repeated reading" or "rereading"), which is effective in improving word recognition, fluency, and comprehension (Dowhower, 1989; Sindelar, Monda, & O'Shea, 1990). Modeling and feedback are important components of repeated reading. Students can listen to an expert and follow along with the print. Then they can repeat the text (echo reading) or read along with the expert reader (choral reading). Students can practice orally rereading in many ways, including choral reading, tape-assisted reading, partner reading, buddy reading, and reader's theater. Ruth Lynn found that repeated reading should be done with short, whole texts (50–200 words, depending on the student) and that poetry is especially well suited because it contains rhythm and rhyme, making practice easy, fun, and rewarding (Worthy & Broaddus, 2002).

Step 3: Ruth Lynn Develops Specific Questions.

Ruth Lynn wanted to incorporate the ideas she learned about in her inquiry with what she was already doing in her classroom. She wrote, "Since poetry is a unit of study in my classroom, and I know that repeated reading is helpful to students in developing fluency, I decided to create a repeated reading program using poetry." Here are her questions:

Teacher-as-Learner Question
How can I design a repeated reading program
to help my students develop fluency?

Student Learning Question
Will repeated reading improve my students' oral reading fluency?

Step 4: Ruth Lynn Creates a Plan.

Setting Goals

Ruth Lynn took a step back to set goals for her instruction. She wrote, "I wanted to design instruction where I could show students what to do and have them pick it up and do it without my constant help. That meant I really needed to think about my goals and what I would need to accomplish them." She set these goals for herself:

- To help students increase their reading rate and accuracy
- To help students develop more interesting oral reading—to read with expression, intonation, phrasing, and prosody
- To teach students to assist one another in meeting these goals

Planning Instruction

Ruth Lynn selected a variety of poems that contained 150–250 words and that would be interesting and appropriate to her third graders. She chose lots of poems, but narrowed her choice to the seven listed in Table 8.1 (one poem for each week of her research). She decided to work with each poem for an entire week. This would give her one day to introduce the poem, three days for students to practice with their partners, and one day for end-of-the-week record keeping.

Table 8.1 Ruth Lynn's Chosen Poems

"Too Many Daves" (214)
From *The Sneetches and Other Stories*, by Dr. Seuss
"Michael O'Toole," by Phil Bolsta (207)
From *Kids Pick the Funniest Poems*, edited by Bruce Lansky
"A Sliver of Liver," by Lois Simmie (163)
From *On Common Ground*, edited by Gerry George, Don Stone, and Faye Ward
"Sick" (208)
"The Crocodile's Toothache" (170)
"Snowman" (211)
From *Where the Sidewalk Ends*, by Shel Silverstein
"A Snake Named Rover," by Maxine Jeffris (244)

Note: The number of words in each poem is in parentheses.

Planning Logistics

As Ruth Lynn learned in her literature review, modeling is critical in helping students recognize and become fluent readers. But modeling fluency was only one part of what Ruth Lynn needed to do. To ensure that she met her third goal, students assisting one another, she needed to introduce the concepts and language necessary for the students to discuss fluent reading, to model the tasks students would do, and to provide them practice in doing them. This part of Ruth Lynn's planning is in Table 8.2.

Planning Data Collection

Although all students participated in the repeated reading instruction, Ruth Lynn decided to collect data from a portion of her class. This would be easier to manage, and looking at a smaller group representing her class as a whole would give Ruth Lynn the information she needed. She chose to collect data on nine of her twenty-four students based on their reading performance: three struggling readers, three grade-level readers, and three above grade-level readers.

Table 8.2 Materials and Mini-Lessons Needed for Ruth Lynn's Project
to Flow Smoothly

Materials to gather:

- Stopwatches (one for every student pair)

Materials to create:

- Time record sheet (first reading, final reading)

- Oral reading rating sheets and rubrics: Cooperative Repeated Reading Response Form from *The Fluent Reader* (Raskinski, 2003, p. 5)

- Copies of poems for each student

Instructional mini-lessons to create:

- What is fluent reading? What are *expression, pace, chunking,* and *accuracy*?

- Why is fluent reading important?

- What does fluent reading sound like? What does it NOT sound like?

- If we are listening to someone read and thinking about fluency, what are we listening for?

Logistical mini-lessons to create:

- How do we use a rating scale or rubric?

- How do we rate someone else's reading (practice w/teacher's reading then each other's)?

- How do we use a stopwatch?

- How do we time someone's reading and record the data?

- What kind of feedback do we give to our partners?

Classroom Research Tip #5
Think about starting small.
Classroom research does not have to include all students
in your class. It might be easier to focus on a smaller group.

Ruth Lynn felt that measuring her first goal (increasing rate and accuracy) was straightforward. She wrote, "I expected that by practicing (rereading) the poems, students would improve their reading rate of each poem each week, and that would be obvious for me to see from the weekly time sheets. That was all well and fine, but what I really wanted to know was whether the improvement would transfer to text students had NOT practiced." In addition to the pre- and post-rates of each poem each week, Ruth Lynn chose to use the DIBELS oral reading passages for Grade 3 as a pre- and post-instruction measure to gain an overall sense of reading rate for novel passages. She could compare students' rates to what is expected in the state's Grade Level Expectations.

To assess her second goal (expressive reading), Ruth Lynn taught students to complete an evaluation of a partner's oral reading. She used the Cooperative Repeated Reading Response Forms (Rasinksi, 2003, p. 92), where students rated their partners' reading on a 1 to 5 scale (outstanding to fair) for decoding (reading the words correctly), pacing (good pace and adjusts when appropriate), and expression (expressive reading in appropriate phrases).

Ruth Lynn planned to assess her third goal (cooperative assistance) by monitoring the buddy pairs and taking notes about the kinds of questions and discussions she heard. She also created a short post-instruction response form for students to share their thoughts about the instruction and their reading.

Table 8.3 Ruth Lynn's Five-Day Poetry Reading Cycle

Monday (thirty minutes) Introduction	Teacher • Model fluent reading by reading poem several times • Discuss poem, explain confusing vocabulary • Echo read poem with students Students • Read poem to partner • Time partner's reading and record time • Complete reading rubric (Cooperative Repeated Reading Response Form)
Tuesday, Wednesday, Thursday Repeated reading (twenty minutes)	Students • Read and reread the poem with partners • Provide input to partner's reading (verbal and in writing)
Friday Record keeping (twenty minutes)	Students • Read poem to partner • Time partner's reading • Complete reading rubric

Step 5: Ruth Lynn Implements Her Plan and Collects Data.

Once students were familiar with the concept of fluency and had sufficient practice in using a stopwatch and rating scale, Ruth Lynn began the repeated readings instruction using a five-day-per-poem schedule, as shown in Table 8.3.

Collecting the Data

Ruth Lynn administered the DIBELS oral reading fluency to the nine target students just prior to beginning the repeated reading instruction, and again after eight weeks of instruction. She collected all Cooperative Repeated Reading Response Forms each week, as well as the Monday and Friday reading rates. She asked students to complete the Poetry with a Partner Response one week after her data collection ended.

Figure 8.1 Average Reading Rate on Monday and Friday Poetry Reading Across Weeks

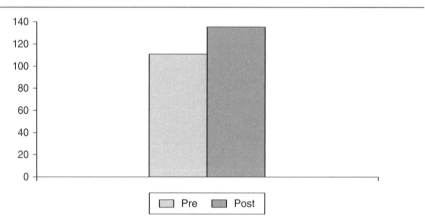

Figure 8.2 Average Reading Rate on the Dibels Oral Reading Fluency Task, Pre- and Post-Instruction, Measured in Correct Words Per Minute

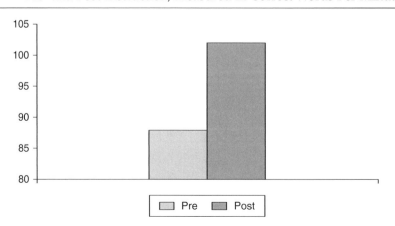

Step 6: Ruth Lynn Analyzes Her Data.

Reading Rate

Ruth Lynn charted students' pre- and post-instruction reading rates from the DIBELS and the Monday and Friday timed rates. Students made lots of progress in reading rate over the course of this eight-week project. Poetry reading rates (according to partners' timing) increased from Monday to Friday by 24 Words Per Minute (WPM) on average across the weeks. The DIBELS oral reading rates increased by 14 Correct Words Per Minute (CWPM) from the beginning to the end of the project (see Figures 8.1 and 8.2).

Quality of Oral Reading

Ruth Lynn found the Cooperative Repeated Reading Response Forms a little trickier to analyze. They were just as much a measure of how well the listener could evaluate the partner's reading as they were of the partner's actual reading. However, she made some interesting observations of how students were integrating their discussions of fluency and refining what they considered "good" reading. During the first week, students rated each other high on decoding, pacing, and expression. The average rating was 2 on a 5-point scale (1 = outstanding, 5 = fair). However, as the weeks went on, students began giving each other ratings of 3 or 4, and, in a few instances, 5. Across the weeks, the above-grade students received the highest ratings and the struggling students received the lowest ratings. Partners rated Friday readings consistently higher than Monday readings across categories.

Teacher Observations

Ruth Lynn quickly came to realize that students were engaged, motivated, and able to assist one another. Her anecdotal notes confirmed this. Here are comments she heard from students:

- "I'm going to go and practice my expression today."
- "No, you need to read it like this. [Demonstrates.] Do you see the commas? You are supposed to make your talking stop for a second."
- "Get some action in your voice, like this [exaggerates pronunciation]."
- "[Kathy], it's boring the way you say it." Kathy: "OK. I'll try it again."

Feedback About the Project

On the Poetry With a Partner Response form, students wrote that repeated reading helped them with expression, rate, and decoding, showing that they integrated these target areas into their understanding of fluent or "good" reading. Here are examples of students' comments about each topic:

Expression

- "I'm using my voices more and if you have good exspren you have better paceing."
- "It helped me with my expreshon and how I read."
- "When we started this I didn't use good expression. But now I do."

Pacing and Rate

- "I got more words read."
- "It helped me read in a very good passie [pace]."
- "I got more reading don when I saterd [started] this."
- "I can stop wen I am aspost to [supposed to]."

Decoding

- "It has hapet [helped] me a lot. I'm a lot bater reader. I understand words bater."
- "I think I am a better reader because I am reading better I can read the words right."

Some students discussed the instruction components (modeling and practice) as being important to them:

- "I didn't know a lot of words but I learned from Mrs. B___ because she reads the poems aloud."
- "I'm a bater read because I have prates [practice]."

Students also reported enjoying the project. Here are some of the things they liked about it:

- "I liked best about this is using my voices because it's fun to use them."
- "I like the powoms [poems] that we get and they realy help."
- "I liked the timming [timing] and doing it."
- "I liked how you get to see how much you can read in a minute."
- "I read with my best friend."

Step 7: Ruth Lynn Reflects on Her Data.

Ruth Lynn could see that her students' rates had increased but was left wondering whether all students' rates increased. She began to think about this with respect to her analysis, so she backtracked.

Reminder!
Compared to What?
Analyzing your data across your whole class
(averaging your data) may hide some interesting
information that can inform your instruction.

Step 6: Ruth Lynn Reanalyzes the Data.

Since Ruth Lynn had deliberately chosen to collect data on a sample of students of varying reading levels, she decided to analyze data for each group of readers (below grade level, on-grade level, above-grade level) separately. A much different picture emerged. The reading rate for the

Figure 8.3 Average Reading Rate Gain of Students at Each Reading Level on the Weekly Poetry Reading Across Weeks

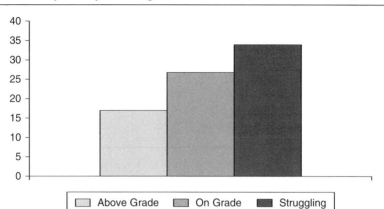

Figure 8.4 Average Reading Rate Gain of Students at Each Reading Level on the Dibels Oral Reading Fluency Task, Measured in Correct Words Per Minute

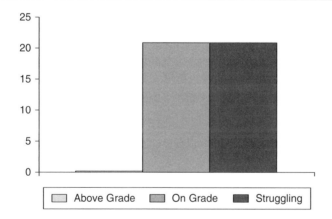

struggling and on-grade readers increased more than the above-grade readers, both in the weekly poetry readings (see Figure 8.3) and on the DIBELS Oral Reading Fluency task (see Figure 8.4). Ruth Lynn also analyzed individual student data to make sure that these averages really did represent her students equally. The total gain for each of the nine students is presented in Figure 8.5.

Step 7: Ruth Lynn Continues to Reflect on Her Data.

Ruth Lynn was pleased with her data. Students sounded more like "good" readers, and their rate increased. But she still puzzled about what it meant—what rate was really "adequate"? Ruth Lynn turned to two

Figure 8.5 Average reading rate gain of each of Ruth Lynn's students on the DIBELS Oral Reading Fluency task, measured in Correct Words Per Minute. Students 1–3 are her struggling readers; Students 4–6 are the average readers; Students 7–9 are the above average readers.

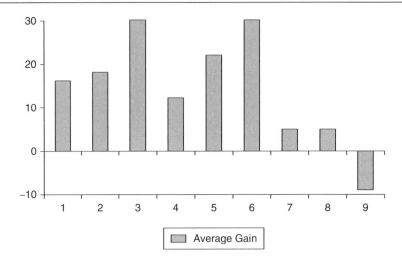

sources for help. According to the *Qualitative Reading Inventory* (Leslie & Caldwell, 2005), typical rate for third graders is 85–139 Words Per Minute (WPM). According to our state's Grade Level Expectations, third graders should read 90–120 Correct Words Per Minute (CWPM). By both of these standards, the above-grade level students in Ruth Lynn's class were already reading at or above a rate expected for third grade. This is why they did not increase their reading rate throughout the project. They were already at the top of the scale. This is called a ceiling effect. That is not to say that the above-grade readers did not gain anything from the project. By their own reports, they learned to use expression better and to monitor their pacing—both qualities of fluent reading.

The on-grade and struggling readers significantly improved their rate. Since Ruth Lynn used CWPM as her measure, she knew the students were not just reading faster, they were reading both faster and more accurately. They also learned a lot about the qualities of fluent reading, as they discussed in their responses and in their conversations with each other during buddy reading.

Although Ruth Lynn's data show that students improved, she felt that there was more to it than the data could show. She wrote, "The students were really motivated to read! We sometimes ask struggling readers to reread, but that sets them apart from the rest of the class. They think, 'Why do I have to read it twice?' This project gave students, regardless of reading ability, a purpose for rereading—to practice 'good' reading—and they all enjoyed it. They were very engaged!"

Step 8: Ruth Lynn Brings Her Research Out of Her Classroom.

Ruth Lynn reported the results of her study to her principal, who was very interested in talking about how this idea could be incorporated into other classrooms. Since Ruth Lynn conducted this classroom research, she has transitioned from a third-grade teacher to an elementary literacy coach. She has also become a staunch supporter of helping students improve their fluency. Ruth Lynn has provided several professional development sessions for teachers about improving fluency. She has also assisted teachers in using repeated reading in their classrooms.

WRAP UP

Ruth Lynn's project helps show that first impressions of data can be misleading. Ruth Lynn's students did made progress as a group, but this was not really the important story. Through cycling through analysis, reflection, and reanalysis, Ruth Lynn was able to pinpoint the improvement. It was not with the students who were already well above expectations for reading with good rate and expression. It was with those students who struggled with reading fluency or who were at the beginning of expectations for their grade.

Ruth Lynn's project also helps frame what is meant by fluency. Fluency is not important just for the sake of reading fast. It is important for comprehension. Think about those students in Ruth Lynn's class who were reading 57 WPM at the beginning of the project. That is less than one word per second. In the long run, these students would be in danger of fluency interfering with their comprehension, particularly when the text they read became more and more challenging and they had less and less background knowledge. Practice does help. Most important, practice rereading the same texts transfers to fluency improvement when reading unfamiliar text.

HOW DOES RUTH LYNN'S PROJECT RELATE TO YOU?

Ruth Lynn's project has two important messages for any teacher. The first message is about data: If data does not seem quite right, maybe it is not. We receive data constantly in schools. Make sure you understand the data and others' interpretation of it. For example, let us say you work in an urban district with many English Language Learners (ELL). The latest test results are in, and local headlines read: "District fails again!" You go on to read how taxpayers' money has been poured into instruction, but students only gained five points over last year. That is probably true, on average. But who gained versus who did not? What were students tested on and in what language? When you ask these questions—when you ask to break down (or disaggregate) the data—the answer is that the ELL students did not make a lot of progress and the English-only students made great progress. You then realize that the ELL students were tested in English, but many were receiving bilingual or ELL instruction. Not only was the data not presented in a helpful way, it was not collected in a valid way. Ruth Lynn's project demonstrates that there may be more to data than meets the eye.

The second message is about fluency: Fluency is important to comprehension. We can work to improve fluency, and if we are not in a position to do that (secondary science teachers probably would not ask students to reread their textbooks), we can model what the text, any text, should sound like. I never really understood Shakespeare until my English teacher read it aloud. When *she* recited Old English, it made sense.

Perhaps the most important take-home message is understanding that fluency, which is really an end product of a long line of lower-level skills, can make or break comprehension. We all need to think a little more about whether students can actually read their textbooks well enough to gain information from them. If they cannot, what is the solution? For older students maybe it is providing adaptations (screen or Web readers) so that all students have equal access to fluent reading. For younger students, we really need to keep fluency on the radar screen of instruction.

YOU TRY IT

Your task in this chapter is to go back to the data that you gathered for your tasks in Chapters 5 and 6. Take another look. Did you find the whole story, or is there something else that can be told?

9

Word Analysis and Phonemic Awareness Instruction for Older Students

---

Classroom Research Spotlight
Steps 3–8: Cycling Through the Process

Literacy Spotlight
Phonemic Awareness

Most children have full phonemic awareness—are able to segment individual sounds in words, blend individual sounds to make words, and manipulate sounds within words—by second grade. But, what if students do not develop phonemic awareness? What happens to them as readers? Can older students develop phonemic awareness? If they do develop it, will it have any impact on their reading ability? These are some of the questions Joell, a middle school special education teacher, struggled with. In this chapter, Joell shares her research into answering some of these questions.

The spotlight for this chapter is the recursive nature of classroom research. This chapter also shows how classroom research can address different goals. Joell and her colleagues had chosen an intervention program for their struggling readers, and her district mandated certain assessments. Joell was able to use her inquiry and her students' data to evaluate the intervention program and the mandated assessments.

JOELL'S RESEARCH

Context for Joell's Project.

Joell's large, suburban middle school, classified as "high performing and improving" is predominantly White of moderate income. The student population is very stable and attendance is good. Fifteen percent of the students receive special education services, and Joell's position is mainly one of pull-out instruction.

Step 1: Joell Notices Her Students' Struggles With Reading.

Over the years Joell had been noticing what her struggling readers could and could not do with reading and writing. However, she was not able to address the issues she saw. She explains, "As a special education teacher, many of the students I see struggle in reading. Because my students are so far behind academically, what I did in the past, and what the teachers wanted me to do, was mainly provide academic support so that students could keep up with their class work. Assessment had not been the driving force for my instruction, and students did not always make gains. In speaking with other middle school special education teachers, the job and the results sounded much the same. We were keeping students afloat but not teaching them to read. So many of my students have word reading problems, which makes it hard for them to access grade-level text. I began to wonder what aspects of word reading gave them trouble (word recognition, phonics, word analysis) and whether they might also struggle with more basic skills, like phonological awareness. If so, I wanted to figure out what I could do about it."

Step 2: Joell Seeks Information to Help Her Students.

Although Joell was interested in lower-level reading skills, including phonemic awareness, she had to inquire more broadly. She needed to think about the impact of lower-level skills on reading ability in general, find information about older, struggling readers, and determine whether going "back to basics" is recommended for older students who need to keep up with an ever-progressing curriculum. Here are some things she found.

Lower-Level Reading Skills Are Critical for Mature Reading

The National Reading Panel (2000) emphasized the importance of five core areas of reading: phonemic awareness, phonics, fluency, vocabulary, and comprehension. The lower-level skills, phonics and phonemic awareness, have great impact on the higher-level skills, vocabulary and comprehension. If word recognition, decoding, and word analysis are not automatic, they disrupt reading fluency, and, as a result, impact comprehension (LaBerge & Samuels, 1974; Wolf & Bowers, 2000). Students who have difficulty reading tend to avoid reading, beginning a reciprocal relationship between reading and learning to read, which Stanovich (1986) termed "Matthew effects"—the rich get richer while the poor get poorer. Those who can read well tend to read more, thereby gaining skills, vocabulary, and background knowledge, which all affect comprehension. Those who cannot read well avoid reading, and thereby do not gain lower-level skills, access to sophisticated vocabulary, exposure to literary language, etc., which serves to create an ever-widening gap between the rich and the poor.

There is a great deal of literature discussing the need for instruction in lower-level reading skills—both phonemic awareness and phonics—in *beginning* reading (National Reading Panel, 2000). There is also research showing that students who struggle acquiring phonemic awareness continue to have reading difficulties through middle elementary school (Juel, 1988). As Joell describes, "This last note, the relationship of phonemic awareness to reading, is something I really thought about for my older students."

What Is Phonemic Awareness?

Phonological awareness is the awareness that speech is made up of smaller units. Speech can be segmented into sentences, phrases, and words. Gradually students understand that words can sound the same (rhyme), start the same at the beginning, and be divided up. Words can be segmented into syllables, syllables can be segmented into individual sounds, and sounds can be blended together to form words. This finest level, isolating and manipulating *individual* sounds in words, is called *phonemic* awareness. Phonemic awareness is crucial to reading development. Children who cannot perceive sound segments will encounter difficulty sounding out words (decoding) and spelling words (encoding) (Beck & Juel, 1995). Students who begin reading instruction with good phonological awareness understand the instruction better, master the alphabetic principle faster, and typically learn to read quite easily. In contrast, those who enter first grade with weak phonological awareness do not respond well to early reading instruction (Torgesen & Mathes, 1998).

Older Students Do Struggle With Lower-Level Reading Skills

In her inquiry into older students, Joell came across something interesting. She wrote, "What struck me most was a tidbit I read on the International Dyslexia Association Web site (http://www.interdys.org), suggesting that 70–80 percent of all students classified as 'learning disabled' have reading problems. That's so high! . . . Many older, poor readers, low-literate adults, and students considered 'reading disabled' have difficulty with phonemic awareness (Torgesen, 1998; Adams, Foorman, Lundberg, & Beeler, 1998). Older, struggling readers also have difficulty using phonic skills to figure out unknown words, and recognizing common words and word parts automatically (Elbro, Nielson, & Petersen, 1994)."

There Is a Lot of Research About Effective Instruction for Beginning Readers

Children as young as three can participate in reading and singing nursery rhymes, listening to rhyming books and poetry, and other activities that help them "hear" language. Children who know more nursery rhymes at age three tend to have more highly developed phonological awareness at age four and phonemic awareness at age six (Bryant, MacLean, Bradley, & Crossland, 1990). However, students who enter kindergarten and first grade without strong skills in phonological and phonemic awareness benefit from direct, systematic instruction in both phonemic awareness and phonics.

There are many programs to teach phonemic awareness and phonics to beginning readers. The particular program matters less than the criteria that it is systematic (follows a predetermined, logical sequence), direct (teachers teach each concept as opposed to providing an environment where students can intuit the underlying principles), and explicit (teacher clearly explain concepts). Direct, explicit, systematic instruction in both areas is beneficial (Adams, 1991; Blachman, Ball, Black, & Tangel, 1994), and combining hands-on phonemic awareness instruction with letter-sounds is most beneficial (Blachman et al., 1994).

Research even suggests how much instruction is necessary. With regard to phonemic awareness, twenty-five minutes per day for approximately twenty hours total is the average recommended instruction. With regard to phonics, the crucial skills can be taught in Grades K, 1 and 2.

There Is Little Research on Effective Instruction for Older, Struggling Readers

Older, struggling readers face even greater challenges than younger students because they are required to do more advanced reading. Although they cannot read well, the curriculum demands solid, grade-level reading skills. There is little research suggesting whether teachers should teach older students the lower-level skills that they did not acquire in the early grades. What exist are mainly recommendations based on what we know about how reading works. Since phonics and phonemic awareness skills are so critical to reading, researchers recommend teaching these skills not only to younger, beginning readers, but to older students who struggle with these skills (Moats, 2001b; National Reading Panel, 2000).

Step 3: Joell Asks Specific Questions.

One of Joell's first decisions was to use her pull-out instruction to target students' reading needs rather provide academic support. She explains,

"Phonological and phonemic awareness have not, in the past, been addressed in my middle school, since these milestones should have been reached by about second grade. Many of our older, poor readers are identified with special needs, yet intervention in reading falls to the bottom of the list, and academic support, homework, and class work become most important. Researching phonological awareness and other beginning reading skills was an extraordinary opportunity. Although I learned a lot, I felt a little frustrated by what I had not learned. How do we know whether our older students have or have not mastered these skills? We certainly don't assess these beginning skills in middle school! What do we do with older students who have not mastered beginning reading skills?" Here are Joell's questions.

Teacher-as-Learner Questions

What are the phonological and word reading skills of my older, poor readers?
If students struggle in these areas, what should I do for instruction?

Student Learning Question

Will a program of direct instruction in phonological awareness
and word study improve reading skills of older, poor readers?

Step 4: Joell Plans Her Assessment and Instruction.

Planning Data Collection

Joell's middle school uses a particular assessment, but Joell was concerned that this would not give her the information she needed to plan her instruction. She wrote, "We are required to give the *Gates MacGinitie Reading Test* (MacGinitie, MacGinitie, Maria, Dreyer, & Hughes, 2000) to all middle school students. This test does well identifying whether students are struggling in vocabulary and comprehension, but it does not assess lower-level skills such as phonemic awareness, decoding, and word recognition. In order to assess these areas, our special education department chose the *Woodcock-Johnson Diagnostic Reading Battery* (W-J III DRB) (Woodcock, Mather, & Schrank, 2006), which has subtests for word identification, word attack, vocabulary, comprehension, and phonemic awareness. Phonemic awareness is measured through Incomplete Words, a task where students listen to a word with a part missing and need to supply the word (e.g., "/a/___/l/" = apple), and Sound Blending, where students listen to a series of individual sounds and blend them into words (e.g., "/c/-/a/-/t/" = cat). Because the W-J III DRB does not assess students' ability to segment phonemes in a word, I chose the *Phoneme Segmentation Screening* from the *CORE* (Honig, Diamond, Gutlohn, & Mahler, 2000), and a benchmark for identifying a need in this area as a score of 70 percent or less."

Planning Instruction

The special needs staff in Joell's district had worked to choose an intervention program for older, struggling readers. They decided on *Corrective Reading* (SRA/McGraw-Hill, 1999), designed to address phonics and word study skills, and *Megawords* (Johnson & Bayrd, 1997), designed for vocabulary building. These were the programs Joell would begin in September.

Planning Logistics

Prior to beginning the instruction, Joell needed to assess students to choose those who needed this type of intervention. Using the *Phoneme Segmentation Screening*, Joell assessed each of her fourteen remedial reading students. Nine scored below 70 percent (six eighth graders, one seventh grader, and one sixth grader). These were the students she chose to participate in the intervention. Joell noted that on the W-J III DRB, her students did better in vocabulary and comprehension than in word reading, which she felt may show that word reading was hampering students' comprehension. Because she also had questions about why the students had such poor word-level skills, she reviewed their records to find out if they were ever identified as having these issues and whether they had received instruction in the early grades. Eight out of the nine students had been identified as having problems in phonemic awareness in elementary school, yet the problems persisted. Either they did not receive appropriate instruction, or they were what some researchers call "treatment resisters" (Torgesen, 2000).

Although Joell had chosen students for the intervention, she still had logistical problems. She wrote, "The schedule in the middle school rotates. Some weeks the students have four reading periods, other weeks they have five. I decided to group the students according to their schedules, rather than their grade. Still, I was not able to create all small groups due to the busy schedule of the middle school, so I needed to see some students one-on-one. I ended up with five groups of students, all of whom participated during their regular school day, except one sixth grader, whom I could not accommodate within any other group. He came after school." Here are Joell's groups:

> Group 1: Three eighth graders
> Group 2: Two eighth graders
> Group 3: One eighth grader
> Group 4: One seventh grader, one sixth grader
> Group 5: One sixth grader (after school)

Step 5: Joell Begins Implementing Her Intervention.

Instruction

In September Joell began the program she and her colleagues had agreed upon—*Corrective Reading* for phonics and word analysis and *Megawords* for vocabulary. She saw each group of students four to five times per week, one hour each session (thirty minutes each of *Corrective Reading* and *Megawords* instruction) from September to the end of January. She also included sight word work periodically.

Step 7: Reflect.

Although she was already implementing her project, keep in mind the classroom research planning mantra: Planning is not static. If I have planned well, but things aren't going well, I can change.

Joell decided to reassess her students mid-year. Although she liked the *Phoneme Segmentation Screening* she had used in September, it was an informal measure so she had no way to compare students' scores on this to their scores on the *Woodcock-Johnson Diagnostic Reading Battery*, or any other standardized measure. Nor could she really know how much progress was "good" progress on the *Phoneme Segmentation Screening*.

Steps 2 and 4: Joell Goes Back to Inquire and Replan.

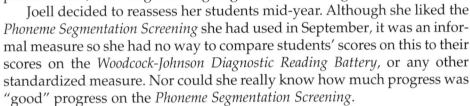

Since Joell wanted a different assessment, she needed to inquire about other measures of phonemic awareness that would be appropriate for middle school students.

She decided to use the *Comprehensive Test of Phonological Processing* (CTOPP) (Wagner, Torgesen, & Rashotte, 2001), a standardized assessment that measures phonemic awareness (phoneme blending and deletion), phonological memory, and rapid naming. She chose to use the phonemic awareness and rapid naming tasks, as she found in her inquiry that rapid naming can also affect lower-level reading skills.

Step 6: Joell Analyzes Her First Round of Data.

Looking at the data from the CTOPP (see Figures 9.1 and 9.2), Joell could see that even though she had been providing students with intensive word analysis intervention for four months, most students were still struggling with phonemic awareness. Her students' scores, on average, were in the low average range for blending words, an easier phonemic awareness task, and almost two standard deviations below the mean in elision (phoneme deletion), a more sophisticated task. Their average standard scores for the phonemic awareness composite was more than one standard deviation below the mean. Her students also struggled with rapid naming, with an average composite score one standard deviation below the mean. Three of Joell's students would not have been identified as "at risk" now based on their CTOPP scores, which could mean that their skills improved since September, but Joell had no way of knowing because she used a different measure with standardized norms.

Figure 9.1 Students' Phonemic Awareness Scores on the CTOPP in January. For elision, students are asked to delete a sound from a word (e.g., "Say bold. Now say bold without saying /b/."). For blending, students listen to sounds and are asked to blend them into a word (e.g., "What word do these sounds make: /m/-/i/-/s/?"). The average range is scores of 8–12.

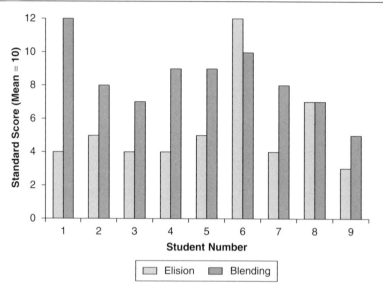

Figure 9.2 Students' Phonemic Awareness Composite Scores on the CTOPP in January. Scores of 85 or below would be considered "at risk." As you can see, three students (Students 1, 5, and 6) no longer are "at risk."

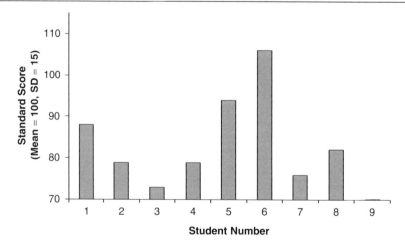

Step 7: Joell Reflects On Her Data and Her Instruction.

While Joell was implementing the *Corrective Reading* program, she also analyzed whether it included explicit phonemic awareness instruction. With the understanding she gained from her inquiry (Step 2), she concluded that it did not explicitly address phonemic awareness. Additionally, the mid-year phonemic awareness assessment showed that most of her students were still struggling to acquire phonemic awareness despite instruction in a structured phonics program. Joell felt her students needed more explicit instruction in phonemic awareness.

Step 4: Joell Revisits Her Plan.

Planning Instruction

Joell decided to add another component to her intervention—explicit instruction in phoneme awareness. She reviewed phonemic awareness programs specifically targeted to older students and chose the *Phonological Awareness Intermediate Kit* (Robertson & Salter, 1997).

Planning Logistics

Although she was adding another component to her intervention program, Joell could not extend students' intervention time and she was mandated to use the chosen intervention programs (*Corrective Reading* and *Megawords*), so she adjusted the instruction to provide all three components into one session: *Corrective Reading* for thirty minutes, *Megawords* for fifteen minutes, and the new *Phonolgical Awareness Intermediate Kit* for fifteen minutes.

Joell taught students using these three programs for eight weeks from February to April. In April, Joell tested her students again, using both the *Woodcock-Johnson Diagnostic Reading Battery* (W-J III DRB) and the *Comprehensive Test of Phonological Processing* (CTOPP). However, since she was using the CTOPP, a standardized measure of phonemic awareness, she did not readminister the phonemic awareness tasks (Segmentation and Incomplete Words) of the W-J III DRB, which she had given in September.

Step 6: Joell Analyzes Her Second Round of Data.

Students' average pre- and post-intervention results for both the W-J III DRB (September and April) and the CTOPP (January and April) are presented in Figures 9.3 and 9.4. Students made great gains in phonemic awareness skills, which were the focus of Joell's research question. Throughout the intervention program, students made good strides in other areas as well. Although students began the program below average on the W-J III DRB, they ended in the average range for most subtests. Their greatest gains were in word attack and comprehension. Their scores in word identification and vocabulary were not as great.

Figure 9.3 Students' Pre- and Post-Intervention Scores on Each Subtest of the *Woodcock-Johnson III Diagnostic Reading Battery*

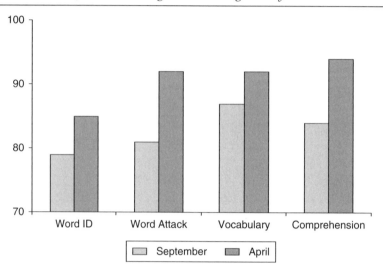

Figure 9.4 Students' Pre- and Post-Intervention (January and April) Scores on Each Composite of the *Comprehensive Test of Phonological Processing (CTOPP)*

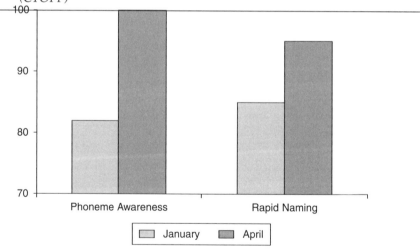

Step 7: Joell Reflects On Her Data.

Although her students' gains were impressive overall, they varied, and Joell needed to think about the relationship of the gains and the programs she was implementing. First, mid-year data showed that students' phonemic awareness skills had not increased with the first phase of the intervention program; April data showed that they made wonderful gains after Joell added a structured phonemic awareness component. Second, phonemic awareness and phonics are related—boosting one may have helped boost the other. Third, students' solid increase in comprehension was most likely a result of their better ability to break words down and get them off the page, since she did not target comprehension in the intervention program.

Although she was not focusing on vocabulary for her research, Joell's intervention did include a structured vocabulary component (*Megawords*). However, students did not make great gains in vocabulary. In reflecting on this, Joell tried to take assessment and instruction perspectives. From an assessment perspective, two things occurred to Joell. First, she was using a standardized measure of vocabulary, with norms adjusted for grade. A standard score that remains the same means that a student has gained expected progress in a year's time. Any standard score gain then is progress above and beyond what would be expected in a year. Second, assessing vocabulary is very difficult. Typically, we don't see progress on standardized measures because vocabulary knowledge is so dependent upon what words are taught (National Reading Panel, 2000). There again, any standard score gain is progress. From an instruction perspective, Joell thought that perhaps *Megawords*, which includes work on syllabication, spelling, and vocabulary combined, had more effect on increasing students' word attack and decoding than it did on increasing their word meanings and strategies for gaining word meanings.

Although she could make sense of most of her data, the variation in students' scores was still nagging at Joell.

Step 6: Joell Returns to Reanalyze Her Data.

Joell looked at each task to note gains made by students who struggled versus students who did not struggle with that particular skill. She found that students' gains in vocabulary and word attack was similar, whether they were initially struggling with these tasks or not. However, for all other tasks, students who struggled made considerably more progress than those who did not. Figure 9.5 was a welcome sight to Joell.

Step 7: Joell Thinks About Her New Findings.

Joell's first thought about this latest turn in her data was that they confirmed what she knew but was not always able to accomplish at the middle school—well-crafted intervention targeted to each student's specific areas of need will work! The answer to another of her original questions—Will explicit instruction in phoneme awareness in conjunction with phonics and vocabulary help improve students' reading skills?—was not as clear cut. It depends. Students made gains in some lower-level skills (phonemic awareness, word attack, and rapid naming) and in comprehension, which may be related. They gained some, but not as much in word identification and vocabulary. But overall, students were moving in the right direction.

Joell also thought about strengths and limitations of her program. She wrote, "There were some unexpected benefits. Many students felt that their reading had improved. Attitude and motivation are so important in

Figure 9.5 Students' Overall Gain on Each Task. Bars represent students divided into two groups based on their scores on the pre-intervention assessment. Students who struggled on a particular task (scoring 85 or below on the pre-intervention assessment) are represented by the first bar while students who were "average" (scoring above 85 on the pre-intervention assessment) are represented by the second bar. In general, students who struggled with a particular skill made more gains than those who did not.

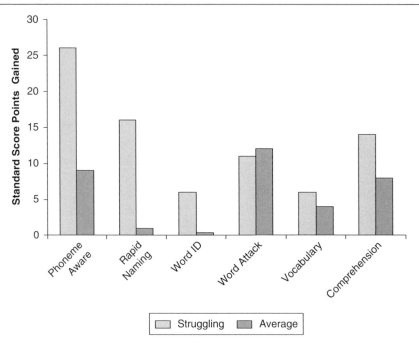

middle school that this is something to think about! Some teachers commented that some of my students were participating more in oral reading in their classes. Along with the benefits though, there were certainly limitations. . . . Unfortunately, I don't think we chose the right vocabulary program for these struggling students—but the program may have helped students' word analysis skills."

Joell learned a great deal about her struggling middle school readers. She wrote, "This experience has been valuable and has shown me that phonological awareness needs to be taught to older students who struggle with it, that it can be taught and have an impact on reading skills, and that it can be fun! There are many games that even older students can play and enjoy while at the same time building crucial skills. Working with older, struggling readers can be very challenging. In addition to what I learned about testing, phonemic awareness, and the ins and outs of intervention programs, I learned how critical it is to build rapport with struggling, older readers. Once my students and I had developed a more trusting relationship, the students were more apt to try out activities that they might have initially felt were babyish or 'stupid.'"

Step 8: Joell Makes Some Decisions for the Future.

Joell's action plan included several important pieces.

Teacher Education

Joell vowed to be an advocate for professional development. She wrote, "All teachers, regular and special education, should be aware of the impact of phonological awareness instruction for young children. The earlier children develop this awareness, the better the chances of becoming successful readers. If only my older readers had received intense, appropriate instruction at a young age! Even still, my students benefited from instruction. I need to make sure that all reading and special education teachers in my school have professional development in this area."

Assessment

Joell and her colleagues made some changes to their assessment plan. She wrote, "If I hadn't assessed phonemic awareness, I wouldn't have known my students struggled. Now we are routinely including a phonemic awareness screen for all of our students who are flagged as struggling readers through the whole-school administered *Gates-MacGinitie Reading Test*. Although the CTOPP might not be practical for us to use as a screening tool (it takes too long), the Phoneme Segmentation Screen that I initially used is quick and can be used as the first layer of diagnostic assessment."

Follow Up

Joell needed to ensure that her students continued to receive instruction targeted to their needs. She discusses her plan: "The data I gained from this project helped me to place my students into what I felt were programs most appropriate for their current needs. Five of my eighth graders will go on to a *Read 180* program [Hasselbring, Kinsella, & Feldman, 1996] next year at the high school. One of my sixth graders, who continued to struggle with phonics skills, will receive Orton-Gillingham instruction [a structured, multi-sensory phonics program]. One seventh and one sixth grader will attend summer tutoring and then stay with me for another year. I'm crossing my fingers for next year's results!"

WRAP UP

Joell's project is a wonderful view into the recursive nature of classroom research. She did not cycle through the steps linearly, but rather as need arose. Joell went from Step 7 (Reflect) back to Step 2 (Inquire). It all depends on what you find and what you need to know.

Joell's project also helps us see that literacy learning is not age-specific. If students do not gain needed skills in the early grades, they need to acquire them in order to make progress. Phonemic awareness is not a skill that middle school teachers think about. However, many older students struggle for reasons that have more to do with primary grade curriculum than middle school curriculum. They may "get" adolescent literature and seventh-grade civics, but they may not "get" how to get words off the page in order to understand the topic. If anything, Joell's project shows us how crucial it is to get at the heart of why older students struggle, so that we can provide them appropriate instruction.

HOW DOES JOELL'S RESEARCH RELATE TO YOU?

There are three take-home messages for all teachers from Joell's research. First, classroom research is flexible and recursive. Second, Joell's research shows that it is possible to adhere to mandates and seek other ways to improve instruction. Joell was required to use particular intervention programs. Yet, with some investigation on her own and creative use of time, she was able to add a needed component and still comply with the mandates. Third, Joell's project attests to the power of targeted instruction. You may not be a special education teacher who can work with students in small groups. But you can think about how you can differentiate parts of your instruction to target what students need, make better use of students' time, and capitalize on your teaching expertise.

YOU TRY IT

Your task in this chapter is to cycle through your own research. Go back to either the literature or to investigate teaching techniques or assessments for your topic area. See what you missed. Perhaps there is something else that you might want to choose, or something you might need to know.

10

Teaching Vocabulary One Part at a Time

Classroom Research Spotlight
Step 1: Notice
Step 3: Ask

Literacy Spotlight
Vocabulary (Morphology)

Angela and Sandy, both middle school teachers, felt that vocabulary was a significant barrier to students' comprehension. Sandy was primarily interested in raising students' vocabulary itself; Angela was interested in working through vocabulary to improve comprehension. However, they both decided on the same avenue of instruction—teaching students morphology, including prefixes, suffixes, and roots. I have put these two research pieces together to spotlight two things. First, noticing what's going on can happen in ways other than observing your current class. Second, even with the same focus of instruction, questions can be different, which leads to different instruction, data collection, and analyses.

SANDY AND ANGELA'S RESEARCH

Context for Sandy and Angela's Projects.

Sandy teaches eighth-grade reading in a "high performing and improving" suburban middle school. This school is predominantly White of moderate income. Twenty-two percent of the students receive special education services. All eighth graders in this middle school take a reading course for one semester. Over the course of the year, Sandy will instruct every eighth grader in the middle school.

Angela teaches seventh-grade English Language Arts in a "high performing and improving" middle school in a suburb next to Sandy's. Angela's school is also predominantly White of moderate income. Seventeen percent of the school's population receives special education services. There are two seventh-grade teams at this middle school, which means that Angela teachers half of the seventh graders.

Step 1: Sandy and Angela Take Different Paths to Noticing.

Although I have talked about Step 1 (Noticing) as carefully observing what you and your students are doing and how you and they are doing it, this is not the only way to understand what is going on. Here are two other ways that Sandy and Angela used to think about their instruction and their students' needs.

Sandy worked six periods a day with eighth graders who she did not already know and who she would teach for only one semester. Taking the time to carefully observe them would mean running out of time. Instead, Sandy took a different approach. She explains, "In the beginning of the school year, I gave my eighth graders a survey to see what they thought about reading. Some of the questions I asked were: 'Tell me two things that you can do now in reading that you weren't able to do before.', 'What would you like to do better as a reader?', and 'What is there about reading that is sometimes difficult for you?' The students' responses were very interesting. They talked about reading bigger words, reading faster, reading more, and understanding what they read. This was interesting to me because last year I noticed that vocabulary was a big stumbling block for my students. I decided to figure out how to help students learn about words."

Angela's noticings came from her experience as a high school English Language Arts teacher the previous year—her knowledge of what her seventh graders would need to do when they got to high school, and what was hard, in general, for high school students. She wrote, "After having spent two years as a high school English teacher, I knew from experience that vocabulary was difficult. I also knew from experience that students seemed to have no strategies for understanding higher-level vocabulary words, which made it difficult for them to fully understand text. I felt that if I could teach students how to unlock the meaning of bigger words—if they could figure out meanings by analyzing the words themselves—they'd have a better shot at understanding what they read."

Step 2: Sandy and Angela Inquire Into Vocabulary.

Sandy and Angela learned several important tenets about vocabulary—that vocabulary is related to comprehension, that teaching vocabulary is possible, and that teaching vocabulary has an impact on students' vocabulary and comprehension. Although they went about their inquiry into vocabulary differently (Sandy started looking at vocabulary structure; Angela started looking at the vocabulary and comprehension connection); they both looked at vocabulary instruction. They ended up in the same place and added yet another tenet to their understanding of vocabulary.

English Isn't Just English!

English words are derived from various heritages. Words now used by many are actually words that previously had been used by few. For example, a word like *schlep*, formerly only used by Yiddish speakers, has become widely used in American English. Word parts from other heritages also make up much of our language. For example, the word *portable* comes from the Latin root *port* (to carry). Approximately 60 percent of English words have meanings that can be predicted from the meanings of their word parts, and the word parts of another 10 percent give useful information to shed light on word meaning (Nagy & Anderson, 1984). That's a lot of words!

Although estimates vary, most suggests that 70–80 percent of English words are derived from Greek and Latin roots. That carries with it good news and bad news. The good news is for elementary teachers. Many Greek and Latin root words are higher-level words encountered by students in the intermediate years and beyond. They probably will not come up in an elementary classroom. The bad news is for upper level teachers. These higher-level words are typically content words. Although they might occur infrequently, they carry much of the content of the reading (Cunningham, 2001). If students do not understand these words, they may be at a loss to understand the texts in which they are used. Most estimates suggest that 80–90 percent of words in science classes are made up of Greek and Latin roots.

Teaching Word Parts Means More Bang for Your Buck

Unlike meanings of isolated words, Greek and Latin root meanings are highly generalizable from one situation to the next (Fry, Kress, Fountoukidis, 1993). In other words, learning one word, such as *biology*, might help you understand your course schedule for tenth grade, but learning one word part—that *bio* means "life"—might help you understand that *biology* is the "study of" life, as well as understand the meanings of *biography*, *biohazard*, and *biosphere*. Researchers in both the fields of linguistics and reading agree that knowing Greek and Latin roots helps students understand vocabulary.

What Word Parts Do I Teach?

Just because we know that word parts are important in learning vocabulary and that we should teach word parts does not mean that all word parts are created equal. Suffixes and prefixes are much more straightforward. Twenty prefixes account for 97 percent of all prefixed words in school texts (White, Sowell, & Yanagihara, 1989), so we know that teaching the top ten of these—or even all twenty—will be helpful. Likewise, the suffixes *s*, *es*, *ed*, and *ing* account for a very high proportion of all suffixed words. Once students learn prefixes and suffixes, they can understand those English words that are related through their morphology (e.g., hunt/hunter, shoe/shoes, dress/undress). These words are *semantically transparent* (Nagy & Anderson, 1984)—the relationship between them is fairly obvious. However, some words are *semantically opaque*, meaning that the relationship is not obvious (for example, the relationship between words like *vice* and *vicious*). We need to help students see the logic in these relationships, but need to be careful. Modern meanings might be very far away from original meanings, so even if we teach root meanings, they may still not make sense to students (Nagy & Anderson, 1984). As Stahl writes, "knowing [the meaning of] *saline* will not help you with *salary*, even though they are both derived from the same root (*sal*). (Salt was once so valuable that it was used to pay workers.)" (1999, p. 48). There is a good list of helpful Greek and Latin roots in Stahl's book, *Vocabulary Development* (1999).

Step 3: Sandy and Angela Pose Their Questions.

As you can see from the questions below, Sandy and Angela wanted two different outcomes for their instruction.

Sandy	Angela
Teacher-as-Learner Question • How can I design instruction to teach Green and Latin roots to my eighth graders? **Student Learning Question** • Will teaching Greek and Latin roots move students up the knowledge continuum for unknown words containing these roots?	**Teacher-as-Learner Question** • How can I teach Greek and Latin root meanings *and strategies to use these roots to figure unknown words in connected text?* **Student Learning Question** • Will teaching Greek and Latin root meanings and strategies help students understand the meanings of words they come across in text? • Will this instruction improve students' text comprehension?

Step 4: Sandy and Angela Plan Their Instruction.

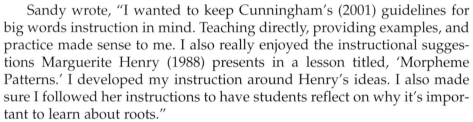

Sandy and Angela came up with different instruction and data collection plans.

Planning Instruction
   Sandy

Sandy wrote, "I wanted to keep Cunningham's (2001) guidelines for big words instruction in mind. Teaching directly, providing examples, and practice made sense to me. I also really enjoyed the instructional suggestions Marguerite Henry (1988) presents in a lesson titled, 'Morpheme Patterns.' I developed my instruction around Henry's ideas. I also made sure I followed her instructions to have students reflect on why it's important to learn about roots."

Sandy used Henry's (1988) and Cunningham's (2001) work to get ideas about instruction. She chose ten roots to teach from two resources she found that contained lists of common Greek and Latin roots:

- *Word Matters: Teaching Phonics and Spelling in the Reading and Writing Classroom* (Pinnell & Fountas, 1998)
- CORE Teaching Reading Sourcebook (Honig, Diamond, Gutlohn, & Mahler, 2000)

She also used the Internet to find good sentences containing the words. She had good luck using *Newbury House Dictionary of American English* (http://nhd.heinle.com).

   Angela

Angela wrote, "I wanted my students to have plenty of opportunity to practice, so I had to consider this when I designed my instruction. I needed to choose a reasonable number of roots and create lot of activities for students to use them."

Angela chose seventeen roots to teach (see Table 10.1) based on *The Reading Teacher's Book of Lists* (Fry, Kress, & Fountoukidis, 1993). To help students learn the roots and practice applying roots to unknown words, Angela created several activities and games, including:

- Greek and Latin Root Discovery Logs for words they came across when reading on their own (see Table 10.2).
- Tally sheet [an idea taken from *Bringing Words to Life* (Beck, McKeown, & Kucan, 2002)].
- Homework: Analyze the root
- *Greek and Latin root Jeopardy* [game adapted from *Words Their Way* (Bear, Invernizzi, Templeton, & Johnston, 2003, pp. 270–273)] (see sample in Table 10.3).

Table 10.1 Angela's Greek and Latin Root List

Root	Origin	Meaning	Word	Definition
cycl	Greek	Circle, Ring	Recycle	Reprocess, reuse, recover
dic	Latin	Speak	Indicative	Points out, suggests
equi	Latin	Equal	Equitable	Fairness, reasonable
fract	Latin	Break	Infraction	Breach, violation
hab	Latin	Hold	Habitation	Dwelling, occupancy
ject	Latin	Throw	Reject	Refuse, throw away, discard
ment	Latin	Mind	Elemental	Basic, simple
path	Greek	Feeling	Sympathetically	Compassion, feeling sympathy
ped	Latin	Foot	Expedite Pedaling	To speed up the process, to work or use the pedals of
port	Latin	Carry	Portrayal	To represent, to depict
sol	Latin	Alone	Insolence	Rude, disrespectful speech or behavior
spect	Latin	Look	Disrespectful	Rudeness, lack of respect
struct	Latin	Build	Instruction	Direction, command
tele	Greek	From Afar	Telegram	Telegraphic message
ten	Latin	Hold	Distended Tenure	Expanded, to stretch out, holding, Possession of
tract	Latin	Pull	Distracted	To draw away, divert
turb	Latin	Confusion	Disturbance	Interruption, disruption

Table 10.2 Angela's Greek/Latin Root Discovery Logs

Directions for Greek/Latin Root Discovery Logs

Please list:

- Any word you encountered and solved through Greek and Latin morphology
- Morpheme used and its meaning
- If the surrounding context was utilized
- Definition of the word that you came up with based upon the above information
- Place where word was found

Example:

- Reporter
- Port (to carry)
- Surrounding context was used as it said, "Sure, the newsreels would roll up, the TV cameras would arrive, *reporters* would hang in the trees, and you'd be famous." I figured that because it said *newsreels and TV cameras arrived* that the word had something to do with the news. *Reporters* seemed like a noun as it said they would hang in the trees. Because of this and my knowledge that the Latin root port means to carry, I was able to generate a definition of the word.
- Report: Person who carries or reports news.
- *My Side of the Mountain* by Jean Craighead George, page 156

Greek and Latin roots that you are being instructed in

Root	Origin	Meaning
Cycl	Greek	Circle, Ring
Dic	Latin	Speak
Equi	Latin	Equal
Fract	Latin	Break
Hab	Latin	Hold
Ject	Latin	Throw
Ment	Latin	Mind
Path	Greek	Feeling
Ped	Latin	Foot
Port	Latin	Carry
Sol	Latin	Alone
Spect	Latin	Look
Struct	Latin	Build
Tele	Greek	From afar
Ten	Latin	Hold
Tract	Latin	Pull
Turb	Latin	Confusion

Table 10.3 Angela's Greek and Latin Roots Jeopardy

Greek and Latin Roots Jeopardy

Procedures:

- The game consists of three rounds: Jeopardy, Double Jeopardy, and Final Jeopardy.
- The player who is selected to go first will choose a Greek/Latin root category and will select a point value.
- An answer will then be read from the category/point value that the player selected.
  Example: Coming from the Latin root meaning, "to look," its definition means "one who watches; an onlooker."
- The first player who responds correctly in the form of a question will add the point amount of the question to his or her total and chooses the next category and point amount.
  Example: What is a spectator?
- An incorrect answer means that points are subtracted.
- When it is time for Final Jeopardy, players see the category, but not the answer. They then decide how many of their points they will risk. When they see the answer, they have thirty seconds to write the question. If they are correct, they add the number of points they risked to their total; if incorrect, that number of points is subtracted from their total.
- The player who has the largest point value at the end of Final Jeopardy is declared the winner.

	Cycl (Circle, Ring)	Dic (Speak)	Equi (Equal)	Fract (Break)	Hab (Hold)
100	A vehicle with two wheels, one in front of the other, and having a saddle like seat for the rider	A reference work containing alphabetically arranged words together with their definitions, pronunciations, etymologies, etc.	Material with which a person or organization is provided for some special purpose	A disconnected part of anything; small portion, fragment	A disposition or tendency
200	A three-wheeled vehicle; especially a vehicle with pedals	The use, choice, and arrangement of words in writing and speaking	Equal in value, force, meaning, effect, etc.	To deflect a ray from refraction	To restore to a good condition

	Cycl (Circle, Ring)	Dic (Speak)	Equi (Equal)	Fract (Break)	Hab (Hold)
300	One who rides or travels by a bicycle, tricycle, etc.	A person having absolute powers of government, especially one considered to be an oppressor	A side of equal length with another	Act of breaking, or the state of being broken	Fixed by or resulting from habit
400	A recurring period of time, especially one in which certain events or phenomena repeat themselves in the same order and at the same intervals	The decision of a jury in action	A state of balance between two or more forces acting within or upon a body such that there is no change in the state of rest or motion of the body	Unruly, irritable	Clothing, attire
500	A system of winds circulating about a center of relatively low barometric pressure, and advancing at the earth's surface with clockwise rotation in the Southern Hemisphere, counter-clockwise in the Northern	Assertion of the opposite of a statement; denial	One of two opposite points at which the sun crosses the celestial equator, when the days and nights are equal	Very low, ragged clouds, slightly cumuliform, which often appear beneath nimbo-stratus clouds during active precipitation	Skillful, dexterous

Answers for Jeopardy

Cycl (Greek)	Dic (Latin)	Equi (Latin)	Fract (Latin)	Hab (Latin)
Bicycle	Dictionary	Equipment	Fracture	Habit
Tricycle	Diction	Equivalent	Refract	Rehabilitate
Cyclist	Dictator	Equilateral	Fracture	Habitual
Cycle	Verdict	Equilibrium	Fractious	Habiliment
Cyclone	Contradiction	Equinox	Fractocumulus	Habile

- *It's All Greek and Latin to Us* [game adapted from *It's All Greek to Us*, found in *Words Their Way* (Bear, Invernizzi, Templeton, & Johnston, 2003, pp. 275–276)]

Planning Logistics
Sandy

Sandy felt that it would be too much to try to implement her instructional plan during each period with every group of students. Because her middle school classes were fairly homogeneous, Sandy decided to target the vocabulary instruction toward the two classes she felt most in need of the vocabulary support.

Sandy also needed to think of time, which is precious in middle school. She taught each class of eighth graders for forty-five minutes per day, which is not a lot of time given all areas she needed to cover. Therefore, she decided that she would devote fifteen minutes of each period to the Greek and Latin root instruction. She created a two-day, two-root sequence of instruction, which is presented in Table 10.4.

Angela

Angela wanted to focus on using roots to figure out new words, so she needed to spend some time making sure the students could transfer root knowledge to new words they came upon in texts. Therefore, she divided her instruction into two three-week segments: instruction (teaching roots and their meanings) and application (how to use roots to figure out unknown words).

Table 10.4 Sandy's Instructional Plan

Day 1 Introduction	Write root on board.
	Read the root and ask students to generate words they have heard that contain the root. Write these on board.
	Have students analyze all words they offered with respect to the root. See if they can come up with a definition of the root.
	Write down the definition of the root.
	Point out the spelling and explain that Greek and Latin roots usually follow regular spelling patterns so they are usually easy to read/spell.
Day 2 Introduce new roots Practice	Introduce new root following the Day 1 sequence.
	Discuss with students the common meanings of these roots and their placement within the words.
	Discuss how using these Greek and Latin roots can be a helpful strategy.

Planning Data Collection

Because Sandy and Angela were interested in two different outcomes (word knowledge and comprehension), their plans for data collection naturally looked different. One commonality, however, was that there was no assessment they could pick up and use. This was one wheel they would need to invent.

Sandy

Sandy wrote, "I wanted to get at vocabulary, but since my instruction was for such a short period of time, I didn't want to only use an all-or-nothing assessment. I also was thinking about the continuum of word knowledge (Dale, 1965) and realizing that my students may end up somewhere on the continuum—maybe they have a general idea of a word meaning, even if it is not precise—and I wanted to capture that."

Sandy created three different tasks using the ten roots she planned to teach to understand students' knowledge of root words under different levels of support. The first task, having students write a definition of each root (e.g., *lum*), provided the least support. The second task, giving students words containing each root (e.g., *illuminate*) and asking them to provide definitions of the words, provided a moderate level of support. The third task, embedding the words in sentences and asking students to define the words, provided the most support.

Angela

Angela also created different assessments to find out what she wanted to know. She explains her decisions: "I really wanted to know whether teaching students how to use Greek and Latin roots to figure out unknown words would help them with comprehension, specifically whether their scores on our end-of-book tests would improve. I had a hard time figuring out how to get at this. If students' scores on the tests did improve, I couldn't be sure that root words were part of that improvement. I decided to include a section on Greek and Latin root vocabulary within the test. That way I could look at vocabulary and comprehension."

To assess vocabulary within text, Angela created two end-of-book tests incorporating a section of ten Greek and Latin root vocabulary words from books the students read in class. The pre-instruction assessment was based on *Nothing But the Truth* (Avi, 1991); the post-instruction assessment was based on *The Giver* (Lowry, 1993). Students had to define the words and provide a sentence for each. To assess what they learned about the Greek and Lain roots themselves, Angela created a simple table with the seventeen roots she planned to teach. For each root, students had to give the origin and definition of the root, a word containing the root, and the definition of that word.

Step 5: Sandy and Angela Implement
Their Instruction and Collect Data.

Using her "two-day, two-roots" plan, Sandy spent approximately fifteen minutes per day with the students talking about roots (about one-third of their instructional period) until she taught all of the roots (about three weeks).

Angela spent three weeks on direct instruction. She introduced the roots, including their meaning and origin, and then discussed various words in which the roots were embedded. She also provided direct instruction and modeled how to use roots to figure out the meaning of unknown words in isolation and in context. Throughout the instruction portion, Angela made practice fun through the teacher-led games she created (Greek and Latin Root Jeopardy and It's All Greek and Latin to Us).

Angela spent an additional four weeks having students apply root word knowledge in conjunction with context clues to unlock the meanings of difficult words appearing in *The Giver*. She had students complete the homework assignments and keep their discovery logs, and began the tally sheet contest.

Step 6: Sandy and Angela Analyze Their Data.

Because Sandy and Angela had different research questions, they needed to analyze their data in different ways. Sandy was interested in vocabulary *knowledge—how much* students knew about the roots. To capture the idea that students might know a little bit, she decided to analyze her vocabulary data based off a modification of Dale's (1965) levels of word knowledge: know it well, know something about it, don't know it. Angela was interested in whether students were *using* Greek/Latin roots to *aid comprehension*. She simply needed to compare students' scores on the end-of-book tests (both the vocabulary and comprehension sections), and the Greek/Latin root tests. Here is what Sandy and Angela found.

Sandy

Sandy's students' responses on the pre-instruction assessments showed that the level of support she provided for the roots mattered. Students could define more words embedded in sentences. They could also define more words than roots. The post-assessments showed that students did make progress (see Figures 10.1 through 10.4), and seemed to be moving up the knowledge continuum from "don't know" to "know it well." However, there were still many students whose written definitions showed that they did not know the meanings of the root words. Although Sandy decided to average students' scores, she noticed that the roots were not all created equal. Students seemed to know some roots better than others, even on the pre-assessment. Students did not know other roots either before or after instruction.

Figure 10.1 Sandy's Students' Knowledge of Roots, Words, and Words in Sentences Represented by the Percentage of Each That Students "Knew Well"

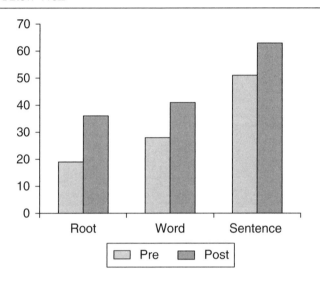

Figure 10.2 Pre- and Post-Instruction Assessment Results for Sandy's Students' Definitions of the Roots, Themselves (Least Scaffolded Task)

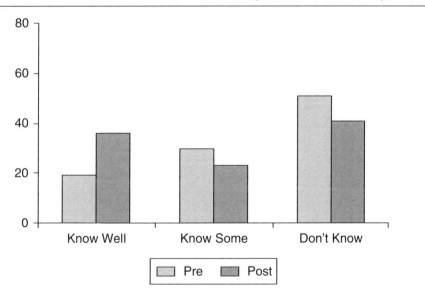

Figure 10.3 Pre- and Post-Instruction Assessment Results for Words Containing Roots (Moderate Scaffolding), Sandy's Class

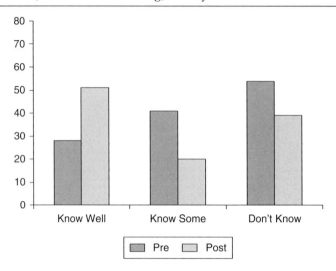

Figure 10.4 Pre- and Post-Instruction Assessment Results for Words in Sentences (Greatest Amount of Scaffolding), Sandy's Class

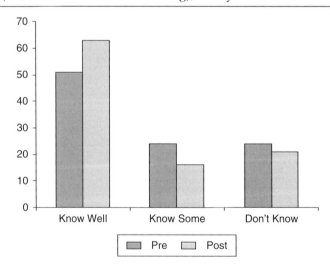

Angela

Angela found that students were already good at providing words containing the Greek and Latin roots on the pre-test and defining those words. However, as Sandy saw, they had a much harder time defining the root itself (pre-assessment average equaled three out of seventeen). Angela noticed that students tried to use the relationship of the word and definition they listed to come up with the root meaning, and that their meanings made some sense. For example, for the root *turb*, several students provided the word *disturb* or *disturbance*, and definitions of "to disrupt," "to bug or enoy [sic]," and "annoyance." These same students defined the root *turb* as "of annoyance, loud," "to enoy or not to enoy" [sic], and "to do something," clearly showing that they were trying to use their word knowledge to come up with root meanings. They were already using a strategy; now they needed to acquire knowledge of root meanings. Angela's pre- and post-test results showed that student were able to do this (see Figure 10.5). Although Angela tried to get at whether comprehension improved, it was just too difficult to determine based on the tests she gave. Angela did find that students improved on the comprehension portion of the end-of-book tests, but not any more than might be typical from test to test.

Step 7: Sandy and Angela Reflect on Their Research.

Both Sandy and Angela, who work in different schools, districts, and grades, noticed students' excitement about participating in the Greek and Latin root instruction. If something came up and Sandy could not get to Greek and Latin roots, students bemoaned, "Aren't we doing Greek and Latin roots today?" Angela was shocked at how much work students put into their Greek and Latin root discovery logs. She had specified the content but not format. To her surprise, students turned in detailed, typed logs, many with cover sheets, page protectors, and bindings. Initially Angela, who was accustomed to high school students, frowned on the idea of games and a tally sheet reward system, thinking students would feel they were babyish. Students loved them.

Sandy and Angela both feel that Greek and Latin root instruction was worthwhile. They also both noted that students need to be actively

Figure 10.5 Pre- and Post-Instruction Results for Angela's Students' Definitions of Greek and Latin Roots

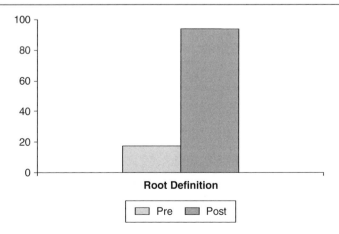

involved in it. Sandy wrote, "My students really didn't know a lot about Greek and Latin roots. I can see improvement even though we didn't spend that much time studying them. But there's a lot I would do differently—including spend more time and get kids more involved! There's just so much else to cover. But I know that students were interested in talking about how these roots and words worked, and I feel strongly that I need to keep incorporating, and even expanding, this kind of instruction for them."

Angela wrote, "I knew students didn't know much about Greek and Latin roots and that was confirmed for me through this research. I originally was going to do this work with high school students, and then I got moved to the middle school. I knew I needed something other than telling students the information and hoping they got it. But games were not my thing—we don't play games in high school. [My professor] kept telling me that [the instruction] needed to be fun, so I made these games even though it practically killed me. What surprised me was how much students enjoyed the project! A lot of that has to do with the activities I set up. I would never have dreamed that seventh graders would be running into the room to tell me that they came across a Greek or Latin root and put their name on the tally sheet, or that they would be so invested in playing Jeopardy! It was so easy to teach them! Not only do I feel students gained a lot of knowledge, I feel that I learned there are other ways [to teach] than standing up there lecturing."

Although Sandy and Angela feel successful in their effort to develop instruction that helps students with vocabulary and comprehension, they both wonder whether students will retain what they learned. They hope they will, or at minimum, that students now understand looking at word parts is a good way to figure out words.

Step 8: Sandy's and Angela's Future Plans.

There are different ways to follow up on a classroom research project. Most important is that you use the information to shape what you do in your own classroom or school. Angela and Sandy both have continued to incorporate Greek and Latin root instruction into their teaching, even though both of them have moved from their respective middle schools. Sandy, who is now a reading specialist at a high school, reports that analysis of word parts is a valuable tool for her struggling readers. Angela, also a high school reading specialist, reports that students need to know how to look into words to help them with their reading.

Reporting your results to someone else (teachers, administrators) is another important part of classroom research. Yet, reporting might not always be practical. Sandy and Angela work in two different worlds with respect to school culture. Angela, as a seventh-grade language arts teacher, was part of a middle school team with the social studies, science, and math teachers. Sandy, as an eighth-grade reading teacher, was in some ways an island.

Reading is a "special" subject, with all eighth graders taking one semester of reading per year. That means Sandy is really not on any team. Where you "fit" with respect to your school community might make reporting to others easier or more difficult. Sandy did not formally share her results with her fellow teachers. She brought up her project and results informally when speaking with fellow teachers, hoping to spark some curiosity and interest.

Angela easily set up a meeting with her seventh-grade team to share and discuss her results and what they might mean for instruction. This led to some interesting discussions. Her fellow teammates began talking about Greek and Latin roots. As it turns out, they all incorporate some instruction within their respective content areas, and according to the state's Grade Span Expectations for seventh grade, students are expected to understand word structure, including roots. But this team had never thought about working together to develop Greek and Latin roots as a common unit of study. Doing so would mean more coherence for the students and less work for the teachers.

WRAP UP

Sandy's and Angela's projects help demonstrate different ways to notice an area of need in the classroom. Neither Sandy nor Angela noticed what their students needed by keeping a journal. Rather, Sandy took her questions right to the students themselves, whereas Angela used her knowledge of what her students would be faced with down the road. These are both valid ways of thinking about what you might want to investigate. In addition, just because we have the same area of interest does not mean we will come to the same place with respect to what we want to do. Sandy and Angela looked into different sources of literature, came up with different questions, and planned different instruction.

In terms of literacy learning, there are two take-home messages from these projects. First, we cannot teach every word that students will need to know. However, teaching older students how to unlock word meanings is a powerful tool to help them create what Clay (2001) terms *self-extending* systems—to help them learn to learn on their own. Because Greek and Latin roots have such generative power, a little knowledge ends up going a long way. Second, students enjoy learning how one word part can go into so many different words. Vocabulary can actually be fun!

HOW DO SANDY AND ANGELA'S PROJECTS RELATE TO YOU?

Classroom research is a process that each of you will go about differently. That Sandy and Angela investigated the same topic does not mean they did so in the same way or that they cycled through the classroom research steps in the same way. They did not. Engaging in classroom research is very personal. You create your research based on your questions and your situation. There is no one "right" way to go about the process. The main point is that you do engage in the *process* in a systematic, reflective way.

With respect to literacy, as we learned from Jayne in Chapter 7, vocabulary is so important! We cannot afford to forget about vocabulary, no matter what age or subject(s) we teach. Jayne, Sandy, and Angela showed us different ways of how to engage students in vocabulary learning, but the outcomes were the same. Students learned vocabulary and enjoyed themselves in the process. Vocabulary is vocabulary—everyone uses it and everyone needs it. These projects help us see that everyone should teach it!

YOU TRY IT

These are the last tasks you will engage in for this book, but hopefully, they are just the beginning of your own project. Here is what you will do:

Classroom Research Task.

Regardless of your own research topic, go to Step 2 and investigate some vocabulary instruction techniques that would be appropriate for you and your students. Try to find one or two things you can add to your repertoire of teaching strategies.

Literacy Task.

Try out the techniques you found in your inquiry into vocabulary. Make yourself include vocabulary as an integral part of your instruction.

11

Ethics and Other Issues in Classroom Research

Classroom research is personal. It is a way for you to analyze and improve your own practice. However, part of your action plan (Step 8) might be to share your research with others, perhaps through offering professional development to other teachers, creating a presentation for administrators, or writing and submitting an article for publication. These are wonderful ways to help others see what you have seen through your research. To use data from your students for any purpose other than to inform you own instruction, though, you must have informed consent from the students' parents. This chapter focuses on these types of ethical issues and also provides you with some suggestions for presenting your research to a broader audience.

INFORMED CONSENT

What Is Informed Consent?

Informed consent means that either the participants in your research (if 18 or older) or the parent(s) or guardian(s) of your research participants understand their or their child's participation in your project. Typically, informed consent includes you explaining in writing what your research is about, what you will be doing with participants, what information you will gather from or about the participants, and what you will do with the information. Then you ask for permission to include the person as a participant.

Informed consent also means that you write your explanations and request in a language that those granting permission can understand. We become accustomed to speaking in education language. We use acronyms and vocabulary that is not typically heard outside of schools and assessment jargon. Informed consent means that you *inform* people—you explain in their language, whether that language is literally another language (Spanish, Chinese) or whether that language is that of someone who does not work in a school.

When Do You Need Informed Consent?

Most often you are conducting classroom research for yourself, and the information you gain is staying with you. In that case, you do not need informed consent. Your research is part of your classroom instruction—part of what you do every day. If your school requires assessments that you will give as part of your research and faculty typically share results at meetings, you would not need consent to bring your students' data. When you are deviating from what is typically done in your school, you most likely need informed consent. All teachers in my classroom research course must obtain informed consent from their students' parents or guardians because I will be seeing the data, even though I might never know the students' names or which names go with which data. Likewise, if a teacher wishes to write up a classroom research project for a local newsletter or a national publication, informed consent is needed. It is best to err on the side of caution. Put yourself in the shoes of participants or parents. Would you like to know that your data has been used this way?

Do Schools Have Policies Regarding Research?

Many school districts do have their own research review boards. Submitting your information to these boards is usually necessary only when what you are doing deviates from what your school typically does. You will find that large, urban districts located near a college or university typically have their own research review boards. This is because colleges and universities regularly request to conduct research in these schools. The research review boards serve to protect the students and their families. Although colleges and universities are usually asking to conduct more formal research, some school districts will require their own teachers to follow the same procedures for classroom research that might be shared with others. If you are unsure whether your district has its own research policies, check with your principal.

How Do I Write an Informed Consent Letter?

There are certain pieces of information needed in an informed consent letter.

- What you will be doing (the instruction, program, or procedure)
- What you will ask participants to do
- What data you will gather from or about the participants
- How you will use this data
- With whom you will share the data

Figure 11.1 is an example of an informed consent letter.

Figure 11.1 Sample Parent Permission Letter

DATE: _____

Dear _____ ,

I am trying to figure out how I can best teach my students to understand the social studies text-books we read. This year I will be working with students in small groups, teaching them how use comprehension strategies, including making predictions about what they will read, asking them-selves questions as they read, figuring out confusing parts of reading, and summarizing what they read. This strategy program is called *Reciprocal Teaching.*

I would like conduct classroom research to see how students do with *Reciprocal Teaching.* I would like your permission to include your child in my research.

For this research I will:

- Give the students the *Stanford Achievement Test (SAT)* to see how they understand what they read. We give this test already, so this is not something new for my project.
- Teach students how to ask questions, summarize, clarify, and predict to help them under-stand what they read.
- Tape record some of our discussions about the textbooks we are reading.
- Type out (transcribe) what students say.
- Use the transcripts to figure out how students are learning the strategies.
- Give students the *SAT* test again in May.
- Look at the two *SAT* tests (September and May) to see how much progress the students made.

I will write a report for my principal, talking about what I did and how my students did. I might also write a paper for a newsletter or journal so that other teachers can learn about this project. If you give permission, I will include your child's test scores and discussions in my report. I will talk about what (HIS OR HER) skills were like at the beginning and end of the project. I will NOT put your child's real name in the paper. If you want a copy of the report, I would be happy to give one to you.

Please complete the form below to say whether or not you will let me use information about your child as part of my research. Whether or not you allow me to use your child's information (HE/SHE) will still participate in *Reciprocal Teaching.* Please return the form back to school in your child's home activity folder as soon as possible.

Thank you for considering my request.

Sincerely,

Sixth-Grade Teacher

Your Child's Name _____

Please check one then sign and date below:

☐ **I agree** to have my child participate in (TEACHER's) *Reciprocal Teaching* project. I understand that (TEACHER) will use my child's *SAT* results and discussions of texts. I understand that (TEACHER) will write a report based on this information and share this report with her principal and other teachers and perhaps submit the report for publication. I realize that my child's real name will not be used in any report or discussions, so that no one but (TEACHER) and I will know that my child is participating.

☐ **I do not agree** to allow (TEACHER) to use information about my child in a research pro-ject on *Reciprocal Teaching.*

Parent/Guardian Signature   Date

X_____   _____

What If My Students' Parents Will Not Give Consent?

If parents do not grant permission for their children to participate, you must honor their wishes. Using data from students whose parents have either not responded to an informed consent letter or who have refused consent is unethical and violates the code of conduct for conducting research. You will still continue with your research and include these children in whatever instruction you are providing, since it is part of your regular classroom instruction. You can also assess all students, if the assessments used are ones you are using as part of your regular classroom assessment. If you share your research with people outside of your school, you simply base your information on the students whose parents did grant permission and exclude data of those students whose parents did not. If you write up your results, you then explain to your readers that you are presenting data from some of your students (usually stated in numbers or percents, such as twenty out of twenty-four students, or 85 percent of the students).

Ideas for Gaining Informed Consent.

There are several things to think about when attempting to gain informed consent. First, check your letter again for parent-friendly language. Try to read it with a parental eye. Second, in your letter you will give parents two options—to allow the child to participate or not to allow. If you do not receive a consent form back from a parent, this does not necessarily mean that the parent is refusing permission. An unreturned consent form might many things. The student could have lost it before even getting it to the parent; the parent could have misplaced it; the parent could have put it in the "need to do" pile and simply forgotten about it. Third, schools send home mounds of paper to parents! Think about how you can get your letter to rise to the top of the heap. The easiest way to gain consent might not be the quickest way. I find that if I call parents first to tell them that the consent is coming home and give them a quick run-down on the project, I get the consent forms back. More work upfront pays off. If I do not get the forms back, I call to remind parents.

If you work with students whose families do not speak English, it is still your responsibility to inform the parents. Many urban districts that serve students from diverse language backgrounds have translation services. If the district does not, the city usually does. Check with the district to find out. Also keep in mind that some parents have low levels of literacy, particularly parents from countries where education is a privilege rather than a right. In those cases, I talk with parents, explain the letter, explain the project, and ask if they feel comfortable signing their consent. If I do not speak the language, I have someone who can speak it interpret for me.

OTHER ETHICAL ISSUES

Choosing Students to Include.

Ideally your project will focus on your class as a whole, or a group of students you feel would benefit from the particular instruction you will provide as part of your research. Making decisions based on pragmatics (Can I teach everyone? If not, who is most in need?) is acceptable. However, excluding a student or students for other reasons is not. For example, let us say that you are using your research to argue for materials or some other type of benefit to your classroom. It would be helpful to show that your instruction is "working." To do so, it might be tempting to only include students who you know will do well. This is not ethical. You cannot make decisions about who to include based on who will give you the best results. That was one of the criticisms of testing that No Child Left Behind sought to guard against—that test scores were artificially inflated because "special needs" students were being excluded.

Telling It Like It Is.

Sometimes our projects simply fall flat. For whatever reason—poor choice of instruction or target area, poor planning, inability to put in the time needed, etc.—we do not see improvement in our teaching or our students' learning. That is part of the classroom research process. If you try a new technique and it doesn't work, change your thinking of what works. Investigate what you are doing and what your students are doing. Move through the reflection cycle to learn what your data are telling you, rather than what you want them to tell you. Present the data as they are, and try to understand them. Sometimes finding that something is not true is equally as interesting as finding that something is true. For example, a teacher had collected and analyzed data about teachers' practices in a particular area, expecting that teachers who held certain beliefs would engage in certain practices. But that was not supported by her data. What she found was that teachers, regardless of beliefs, did not have a common understanding of the particular topic, nor did they really instruct it. This was important. However, because this teacher approached her data with a preconceived notion about the results, it was hard for her to see that what she did not find was very telling.

GAINING HELP WITH CLASSROOM RESEARCH

Sometimes the project you want to undertake requires support, whether it is funding, people, materials, or other. Check with your district and community. Perhaps there is funding available for a project like yours. For example, Joell, from Chapter 9, did not own the phonemic awareness assessment she chose to give, nor did her district. It was expensive, and she did not want to purchase it on her own. She went online to her district, town, and community Web sites and found many sources of grant money for educators. She wrote the grant for the funds to purchase the assessment.

There are also outside sources of funding for classroom research in literacy. The International Reading Association sponsors the Teacher as Researcher Grant of up to $5,000 to teachers who conduct classroom research in literacy (see http://www.reading.org/association/awards/research_teacher_as_researcher.html). Other organizations also offer support for teachers conducting classroom research.

A listing of some of these is in Table 11.1.

DISSEMINATING CLASSROOM RESEARCH

There are many forums in which you can report your classroom research to others. Some of these include

- A teacher or school personnel presentation or professional development session
- A local or national conference presentation
- A school or district newsletter article
- A district administration report
- A teacher journal or magazine piece
- A research journal report
- An Internet teaching site write-up
- A parents' summary
- A university paper (course paper, master's or doctoral thesis)

If you choose to write up your project, you will need to follow conventional guidelines for writing research. If you have followed the classroom research process outlined in this book, you have all of the necessary

Table 11.1 Suggestions for Classroom Research Funding

Organization or Resource	Contact Information
Teachers Network	http://www.teachersnetwork.org/
School Grants	http://www.schoolgrants.org/
NEA Foundation	http://www.neafoundation.org/grants.htm
TeacherResearch.Net	http://www.teacherresearch.net/rm_bids4funding.htm
National Council of Teachers of English (NCTE)	http://www.ncte.org/about/grants

Table 11.2 Classroom Research Steps Mapped to Typical Sections in a
Journal Article

Classroom Research Step	Journal Article Section
Step 1: Notice	Introduction (statement of the problem)
Step 2: Inquire	Literature review (theoretical rationale)
Step 3: Ask	Research question(s)
Step 4: Plan Step 5: Implement	Method
Step 5: Implement Step 6: Analyze	Data collection Data analysis Results
Step 7: Reflect Step 8: Plan	Discussion

components to write up your research in a conventional way. Most literacy journals adhere to the guidelines of the *Publication Manual of the American Psychological Association* (APA). In Table 11.2, you will find a map of how the steps of classroom research align with what is expected in a typical journal article. How to write up this information and what to say depends on the journal. Reading the journal you wish to target gives you an idea of how articles in that journal are put together.

WRAP UP

Ethics in research are so important. If teachers and school personnel want to be respected as researchers they need to abide by the same set of ethical principles. As a teacher, administrator, or other school employee, you know the importance of communicating with parents. Research ethics are equivalent to good communication with parents.

CONCLUDING COMMENTS

I hope you are now ready, have already begun, or have even completed your own classroom research and that this book has given you the tools to do so. Becoming a researcher is a process that all teachers, administrators, reading specialists, and other professional personnel can undertake. I encourage you to try classroom research, to collaborate with your colleagues around conducting classroom research, and to share your research with others. Classroom research truly does make a difference. By undertaking it, I hope that you will learn about your teaching and about your students' learning and that you will become a spokesperson for the importance of classroom research.

Resource A

Practice Open-Coding

TEACHER 1

Talk about your role in the assessment process in your school and your classroom.

I am the assessor [laughs]. I am the person who has to do all the assessments for my classroom. So I do all of the assessments from the get go. I do a spelling assessment right in the beginning of the school year. I do the DRA [*Developmental Reading Assessment*] to assess their reading levels. I do the Gates [Gates-McGinitie Reading Test] for the assessments; it is also a district mandate. I do a pre-assessment when it comes to mathematics to see where they are. I do a pre-assessment before every unit to see what they know. I create the post-assessment. But now in our district there is a group of teachers that are coming out with different post-assessments for all of our units, so now they created them. But I am the one in charge of doing all the assessments. Our literacy specialist will come in and help us do the DRA because we have so many kids that struggle. There is a lot more that goes into the tests when they are there because we want to take so many notes, so she comes in and helps us. I am also the one that is responsible for making sure we meet the goals on the PLPs [Personal Literacy Plans], keep them updated, and write the PLPs. So that is all on my lap. Anyone who assists me with those is great, but I am the one who is responsible for all of it.

Talk about how assessment informs your instruction.

It tends to; well, informal and formal drive my instruction. Informal assessments when I am just going around and conferencing with them or just checking their work or the dip stick assessment. That is what drives my instruction. I know what my curriculum is that I have to ultimately teach, but if they don't have some of the basics and I realize that when I

183

am going around looking at their work or watching them in a group with their conferences with each other or when they are conferencing with me, checking out their homework. If they aren't producing or not getting it, then that is what's telling me what to do next. I use assessment quite a bit to help me drive my instruction, but it is not a big formal assessment. I do that, but a lot of informal assessment goes on whether it is conversations or me looking over their shoulders—it drives it. Ultimately I have that goal that I need to complete, but I might need to take a lot more steps to get to it rather than the big leap in other schools. But it drives it—it tells me where to go.

TEACHER 2

Talk about your role in the assessment process in your school and your classroom.

Well, we are required to give the GRADE test [Group Reading Assessment and Diagnostic Evaluation] at the beginning of the year. Any child who has 40 percent or below on that test would get a PLP [Personal Literacy Plan], which is required by our state for any student below grade level in reading. The plan states the child's strengths/weaknesses, and the plan to bring the child up to grade level. So that's kind of what we write the PLPs from. We've been given the WRAP [ORBIT Writing and Reading Assessment Profile] assessment and we've been given the Rigby assessment [Rigby PM Benchmark]. Either one we can use to kind of get an instructional reading level. I like the WRAP because although it takes about twenty minutes per child—not to administer—but to really sit down and evaluate, maybe twenty minutes to a half hour. It's probably one of the quicker ones. . . . The stuff that I learned in the reading program, the assessments that I learned in the reading program, although I think those are better to diagnose a child's difficulties, I don't have the time to administer those. So the WRAP is a close second to those. It's quick. I like to use that. We also this year just got training on the DIBELS [Diagnostic Indicators of Basic Early Literacy Skills] oral reading fluency test. So now we are required to do the DIBELS, just for the oral reading fluency. So those are the assessments that we are required to give. I will use the spelling inventory from *Words Their Way*. But other than that, that would be basically it.

Talk about how assessment informs your instruction.

Definitely, what I get from the WRAP. I get their instructional reading level from the WRAP. I get information from the WRAP; you take a running record. It asks them to do a retell. And then you ask them a couple of questions. So, it kind of follows that QRI [Qualitative Reading Inventory]-type format. So from the kind of retell they give me, the kinds of questions they're having difficulty with, because they'll [WRAP] ask recalling details questions, or synthesizing information, and there's about three or four of them. From those, I'll take what I think they might be having trouble with. So that little girl that I was talking about, she definitely has trouble organizing a retell, so I will work on that, or recalling facts. I will work on that or synthesizing information. A few of the children that I did the running record with had fluency issues; definitely had fluency issues. So I have in my plans this week to use those Dolch word phrases from Timothy Rasinski's book [*The Fluent Reader*] and we're going to do some of those, and we're going to do some timed fluency drills, so that kind of thing. I would take from the WRAP assessment and from the GRADE [Group Reading Assessment and Diagnostic Evaluation] assessment (they break it down into the different components of the assessment) what their strengths are and what their weaknesses are, and what they were average at. I will take those and during that guided reading time I will try to develop the use of graphic organizers, the fluency word lists, or that kind of thing.

Resource B

Text Talk Script:
Officer Buckle and Gloria

Cover:
Read the title and author's name. Tell students that Officer Buckle and Gloria visit schools to share safety tips.

Initial Questions:

- What is a safety tip?
- What safety tips might Officer Buckle and Gloria share with the students in the school?
- Why is it important to know about safety?

Page 2:
Initial Question: What's going on here? (The students are bored, uninterested; not listening.)
Follow Up: The author says, "Sometimes there was snoring." What does this tell us? (The children are bored.)

Page 3: (Show picture)
Initial Question: What do we know? (No one listened so his talk did no good; there were many accidents.)
Follow Up: It was business as usual after the speech. What does this tell us? (No one ever listens to his speeches.)

Page 5:
Initial Question: What do we know about Gloria? (She's an obedient dog.)
Follow Up: What could we say about Gloria? (She's obedient, she listens.)

Page 6: (Show picture)
Initial Question: Oh no, what's going on? (Gloria is demonstrating the safety tip by copying Officer Buckle.)

Page 7:
Initial Question: Why does Officer Buckle check on Gloria? (To see if she's sitting at attention [retrieve] or he's wondering why the children sat up and stared [infer].)
Initial Question: When Officer Buckle looks back Gloria is sitting at attention. What does this tell us about Gloria? (She does not want Officer Buckle to see what she's doing.)

Page 9:
Initial Question: What's going on here? (Gloria is sitting at attention. Officer Buckle does not realize she's tricking him. Officer Buckle does not realize what she's doing.)
Follow Up: Why does Officer Buckle say "good dog"? (He thinks she's sitting at attention. He doesn't realize what she's doing.)
Follow Up: What must Officer Buckle think? (That the students are interested in him.)

Page 10: (Show picture)
Initial Question: Why is the audience roaring? (They are laughing at Gloria. They think she is very funny.)
Follow Up: The audience roared. That means they laughed and cheered really hard. Why? (They think Gloria is really funny. They are laughing at her.)

Page 11:
Initial Question: Why does Officer Buckle say the rest of the safety tips with plenty of expression? (He thinks they are interested in him. He thinks it's him they are laughing at.)

Initial Question: It says, "Officer Buckle had never noticed how funny safety tips could be." What does this tell us? (He still does not realize what Gloria is doing).
Follow Up: Why doesn't he realize this? (He can't see Gloria, and every time he turns around she stops and behaves.)

Initial Question: After this safety speech there wasn't a single accident. Why not? (Everybody was listening.)
Follow Up: What happened before Gloria came along? (No one listened and there were a lot of accidents.)
Follow Up: What happened the last time Officer Buckle gave his speech alone? (No one listened and there were a lot of accidents.)

Page 13:
Initial Question: Every letter had a picture of Gloria. What does this tell us? (The kids really liked Gloria.)

Initial Question: Officer Buckle thought the drawings showed a lot of imagination. What does this tell us about Officer Buckle? (He thinks the drawings were so creative because he still does not realize what Gloria is doing.)

Page 14: (Show picture)
Initial Question: Why do you think this was Officer Buckle's favorite letter? (He was in the picture for once.)
Follow Up: What do you notice about all the other letters? (Gloria is in every picture, not Officer Buckle.)

Page 15:
Initial Question: What's going on? (Everyone is talking about the speech. Everyone wants to hear it.)
Follow Up: What must Officer Buckle think? (Everyone is interested in him and Gloria.)

Page 18:
Initial Question: What's going on? (He's being videotaped by the news people.)
Follow Up: Why? (They are going to do a story on him.)

Page 23:
Initial Question: What will Officer Buckle see on the news? (What Gloria is doing.)
Follow Up: How do you think he'll feel about that? Why? (Shocked and upset because he realizes the children are laughing at Gloria.)

Page 24:
Initial Question: What's going on? (Officer Buckle is not doing any more speeches but the principal wants Gloria to come because she's funny.)
Follow Up: Why does the principal want Gloria to come without Officer Buckle? (She's funny.)

Page 25:
Initial Question: What's happening? (The audience is bored.)
Follow Up: Why? (Gloria is not performing because Officer Buckle is not there.)
Follow Up: It says, "Gloria and the audience fell asleep." What does this tell us about Gloria giving safety speeches? (She needs Officer Buckle.)

Page 27:
Initial Question: What do the accident and Claire's note tell us about Officer Buckle and Gloria's safety speeches? (Kids need and learn from them both. They prevent accidents.)

Follow Up: What happened after Gloria gave the speech by herself? (Napville's biggest accident ever.)
Follow Up: How could the accident have been prevented? (If Officer Buckle and Gloria gave the speech together; people would have listened)

Page 29: (Show picture)
Initial Question: Why does Officer Buckle decide to give safety speeches with Gloria again? (He knows they make a good team.)
Follow Up: Will Officer Buckle go back to doing safety speeches alone? Why? (No, because students listen when they both give the speech.)
Follow Up: What has Officer Buckle learned? (Sometimes it's important to work as a team.)

References

Adams, M. J. (1991). *Beginning to read: Thinking and learning about print.* Cambridge, MA: MIT Press.

Adams, M. J., Foorman, B., Lundberg, I., & Beeler, T. (1998). *Phonemic awareness in young children: A classroom curriculum.* Baltimore, MD: Paul H. Brookes.

Allington, R. L. (1983). Fluency: The neglected goal. *The Reading Teacher, 36,* 556–561.

Anders, P., Hoffman, J., & Duffy, G. (2000). Teaching teachers to teach reading: Paradigm shifts, persistent problems, and challenges. In M. Kamil, P. Mosenthal, P. D. Pearson, & R. Barr (Eds.), *Handbook of reading research, Vol. III* (pp. 719–742). Mahwah, NJ: Lawrence Earlbaum Associates.

Anderson, R., Hiebert, E., Scott, J., & Wilkinson, I. (1985). *Becoming a nation of readers: The report of the Commission on Reading.* Champaign, IL: Center for the Study of Reading.

Anderson, R. C., Wilson, P. T., & Fielding, L. G. (1988). Growth in reading and how children spend their time outside of school. *Reading Research Quarterly, 23,* 285–303.

Avi. (1991). *Nothing but the truth.* New York: Scholastic.

Avi. (1995). *Poppy.* New York: Harper Trophy.

Ball, E., & Blachman, B. (1991). Does phoneme awareness training in kindergarten make a difference in early word recognition and developmental spelling? *Reading Research Quarterly, 26,* 49–66.

Bear, D., Invernizzi, M., Templeton, S., & Johnston, F. (2003). *Words their way: Word study for phonics, vocabulary, and spelling instruction* (3rd ed.). Upper Saddle River, NJ: Pearson/Merrill-Prentice Hall.

Beaver, J. (2001). *Developmental reading assessment: K–3 teacher resource guide.* Parsippany, NJ: Celebration Press.

Beck, I. (1999). *Word Building.* Retrieved on July 19, 2008, from http://www.education.pitt.edu/leaders/decoding/wordbuilding.aspx

Beck, I., & Juel, C. (1995). The role of decoding in learning to read. *American Educator, 19*(2), 8, 21–25, 39–42.

Beck, I. L., & McKeown, M. G. (2001). Text talk: Capturing the benefits of read-aloud experiences for young children. *The Reading Teacher, 55*(1), 10–20.

Beck, I., McKeown, M., Hamilton, R., & Kucan, L. (1997). *Questioning the author: An approach for enhancing student engagement with text.* Newark, DE: International Reading Association.

Beck, I. L., McKeown, M. G., & Kucan, L. (2002). *Bringing words to life: Robust vocabulary instruction.* New York: Guilford Press.

Beck, I. L., Perfetti, C., & McKeown, M. G. (1982). Effects of long-term vocabulary instruction on lexical access and reading comprehension. *Journal of Educational Psychology, 74,* 506–521.

Biemiller, A. (1999, April). *Estimating vocabulary growth for ESL children with and without listening comprehension instruction.* Paper presented at the annual conference of the American Educational Research Association, Montreal, Quebec.

Biemiller, A. (2001). Teaching vocabulary: Early, direct, and sequential. *The American Educator, 25,* 24–28.

Blachman, B., Ball, E., Black, R., & Tangel, D. (1994). Kindergarten teachers develop phoneme awareness in low-income, inner-city classrooms: Does it make a difference? *Reading and Writing, 6*(1), 1–18.

Blachman, B., Ball, E., Black, R., & Tangel, D. (2002). *Road to the code: A phonological awareness program for young children.* Baltimore, MD: Brookes.

Blevins, W. (1998). *Phonics A to Z: A practical guide.* New York: Scholastic.

Bloom, B. (1984). *Taxonomy of educational objectives.* Boston: Allyn & Bacon.

Bond, G., & Dykstra, R. (1997). The cooperative research program in first-grade reading instruction. *Reading Research Quarterly, 32*(4), 345–428.

Brett, A., Rothlein, L., & Hurley, M. (1996). Vocabulary acquisition from listening to stories and explanations of target words. *Elementary School Journal, 96,* 415–422.

Bryant, P. E., MacLean, M., Bradley, L., & Crossland, J. (1990). Rhyme and alliteration, phoneme detection and learning to read. *Developmental Psychology, 26,* 429–438.

Calkins, L. (2000). *The art of teaching reading.* Boston: Allyn & Bacon.

Chall, J. S. (1983). *Stages of reading development.* New York: Teachers College Press.

Chall, J. S., Jacobs, V., & Baldwin. (1991). *The reading crisis: Why poor children fall behind.* Cambridge, MA: Harvard University Press.

Clay, M. (1991). *Becoming literate: The construction of inner control.* Portsmouth, NH: Heinemann.

Clay, M. (1998). *An observation survey of early literacy achievement.* Portsmouth, NH: Heinemann.

Clay, M. (2001). *Change in time in children's literacy development.* Portsmouth, NH: Heinemann.

Cochran-Smith, M., & Lytle, S. (1999). The teacher research movement: A decade later. *Educational Researcher, 28*(7), 15–25.

Cunningham, P. (2001). *Making more big words.* Grand Rapids, MI: Frank Schaffer.

Cunningham, P., & Hall, D. (1997). *Month-by-month phonics for first grade: Systematic, multilevel instruction.* Greensboro, NC: Carson-Dellosa Publishing.

Dale, E. (1965). Vocabulary measurement: Techniques and major findings. *Elementary English, 42,* 82–88.

Daniels, H. (1994). *Literature circles: Voice and choice in the student-centered classroom.* New York: Stenhouse.

Darling-Hammond, L. (1996). The quiet revolution: Rethinking teacher development. *Educational Leadership, 53,* 4–10.

DeGross, M. (1994). *Donovan's word jar.* New York: Harper Trophy.

Dickinson, D., & Smith, M. (1994). Long-term effects of preschool teachers' book reading on low income children's vocabulary and story comprehension. *Reading Research Quarterly, 29,* 104–122.

Dinkelman, T. (1997). The promise of action research for critically reflective teacher education. *Teacher Educator, 32,* 250–74.

Dowhower, S. (1989). Repeated reading into practice. *The Reading Teacher, 42,* 502–507.

Elbro, C., Nielson, I., & Petersen, D. (1994). Dyslexia in adults: Evidence for deficits in non-word reading and in the phonological representation of lexical items. *Annals of Dyslexia, 44*(1), 203–226.

Elley, W. B. (1988). Vocabulary instruction from listening to stories. *Reading Research Quarterly, 24,* 174–187.

Feitelson, D., Goldstein, Z., Eshel, M., Flasher, A., Levin, M., & Sharon, S. (1991). *Effects of listening to stories on kindergartners' comprehension and use of language.* Unpublished manuscript.

Fielding-Barnsley, R. (1997). Explicit instruction in decoding benefits children high in phonemic awareness and alphabetic knowledge. *Scientific Studies in Reading, 1,* 85–98.

Foorman, B., Francis, D., Fletcher, J., & Schatschneider, C. (1998). The role of instruction in learning to read: Preventing reading failure in at-risk children. *Journal of Educational Psychology, 90,* 37–55.

Fountas, I. C., & Pinnell, G. S. (1996). *Guided reading: Good first teaching for all students.* Portsmouth, NH: Heinemann.

Fountas, I. C., & Pinnell, G. S. (2002). *Phonics lessons: Letters, words, and how they work: Grade 1.* Portsmouth, NH: Heinemann.

Fry, E., Kress, J., & Fountoukidis, D. (1993). *The reading teacher's book of lists.* Paramus, NJ: Prentice Hall.

Goldenberg, C. (1993). Instructional conversations: Promoting comprehension through discussion. *The Reading Teacher, 46*(4), 316–326.

Good, R., & Kaminski, R. (Eds.). (2002). *Dynamic indicators of basic early literacy skills* (6th ed.). Eugene, OR: Institute for the Development of Educational Achievement. Retrieved April 20, 2008, from http://dibels.uoregon.edu/

Goulden, R., Nation, P., & Read, J. (1990). How large can a receptive vocabulary be? *Applied Linguistics, 11,* 341–363.

Gray-Schlegel, M. A., & Matanzo, J. B. (1993). Action research: Classroom teachers' perceptions of its impact on the teaching of reading. In T. Rasinski & N. Padak (Eds.), *Inquiries in literacy learning and instruction: The fifteenth yearbook of the College Reading Association.* Pittsburg, KS: College Reading Association.

Greany, K., Tunmer, W., & Chapman, J. (1997). Effects of rime-based orthographic analogy training on the word recognition skills of children with reading disability. *Journal of Educational Psychology, 89,* 645–651.

Hart, B., & Risley, T. (1995). The early catastrophe: The 30 million word gap. *The American Educator, 27,* 4–9.

Hasselbring, T., Kinsella, K., & Feldman, K. (1996). *Read 180.* New York: Scholastic.

Hauslein, C., & Kapusnick, R. (2001). The silver cup of differentiated instruction. *Kappa Delta Pi Record, 37*(4), 156–159.

Henry, M. (1988). Beyond basics: Integrated decoding and spelling instruction based on word analysis and structure. *Annals of Dyslexia, 38,* 258–275.

Hensen, K. T. (1996). Teachers as researchers. In J. Sikula, J. P., Buttery, T. J., & Guyton, E. (Eds.), *Handbook of research on teacher education.* New York: MacMillan.

Hirsch, E. (2001). Overcoming the language gap: Make better use of the literacy time block. *The American Educator, 25,* 28–30.

Honig, B., Diamond, L., Gutlohn, L., & Mahler, J. (2000). *Teaching reading sourcebook: Sourcebook for kindergarten through eighth grade.* Novato, CA: Academic Therapy Publications.

Hook, P., & Jones, S. (2002). The importance of automaticity and fluency for efficient comprehension. *Perspectives, 28,* 9–14.

Information Works! (2002). *SALT survey reports 2001–2002.* Retrieved April 25, 2003, from http://infoworks.ride.uri.edu/2002/pdf/20103M-p1.pdf

Information Works! (2003). *SALT survey reports 2001-2002.* Retrieved April 25, 2003, from http://infoworks.ride.uri.edu/2005/pdf/achievement/36103M-achi.pdf

Johnson, K., & Bayrd, P. (1997). *Megawords: Multisyllabic words for reading, spelling, and vocabulary.* Cambridge, MA: Educator's Publishing Service.

Juel, C. (1988). Learning to read and write: A longitudinal study of fifty-four children from first through fourth grade. *Journal of Educational Psychology, 80,* 437–447.

Kolich, E. M. (1991). Effects of computer-assisted vocabulary training on word knowledge. *Journal of Educational Research, 84,* 177–182.

Kratky, L. (2000). *Hampton-Brown teacher's guide phonics and friends: Level B.* Carmel, CA: Hampton-Brown.

Laberge, D., & Samuels, S. J. (1974). Toward a theory of automatic processing in reading. *Cognitive Psychology, 6,* 293–323.

Leslie, L., & Caldwell, J. (2001). *Qualitative reading inventory* (3rd ed.). Boston: Longman.

Leslie, L., & Caldwell, J. (2005). *Qualitative reading inventory* (4th ed.). Boston: Allyn & Bacon.

Levin, J. R., McCormick, C., Miller, G., & Berry, J. (1984). Mnemonic versus nonmnemonic vocabulary strategies for children. *American Educational Research Journal, 19,* 121–136.

Lewin, K. (1948). Group decisions and social change. In T. M. Newcomb & E. L. Hartley, (Eds.), *Readings in social psychology.* New York: Henry Holt.

Lowry, L. (1993). *The Giver.* Boston: Houghton Mifflin.

Lytle, S., & Cochran-Smith, M. (1990). Learning from teacher research: A working typology. *Teachers College Record, 92*(1), 83–103.

MacGinitie, W., MacGinitie, R., Maria, K., Dreyer, L., Hughes, K. (2000). *Gates-MacGinitie reading test.* Rolling Meadows, IL: Riverside.

Marshall, J. (1997). *Rats on the roof and other stories.* New York: Puffin Books.

McKenna, M. C., & Kear, D. J. (1990, May). Measuring attitude toward reading: A new tool for teachers. *The Reading Teacher, 43*(8), 626–639.

Moats, L. C. (2000). *Speech to print: Language essentials for teachers.* Baltimore, MD: Paul H. Brooks Publishing, Co.

Moats, L. C. (2001a). Overcoming the language gap: Invest in teacher professional development. *The American Educator, 25,* 31–33.

Moats, L. C. (2001b). When older students can't read. *Educational Leadership, 58*(6).

Morrow, L. (1985). Retelling stories: A strategy for improving young children's comprehension, concept of story structure, and oral language complexity. *The Elementary School Journal, 85*(5), 646–661.

Morrow, L. (1990). Small group story readings: The effects on children's comprehension and response to literature. *Reading Research and Instruction, 29,* 1–17.

Nagy, W. (1998). *Teaching vocabulary to improve reading comprehension.* Newark, DE: International Reading Association.

Nagy, W. E., & Anderson, R. C. (1984). How many words are there in printed school English? *Reading Research Quarterly, 19,* 304–330.

Nagy, W., Herman, P., & Anderson, R. (1985). Learning words from context. *Reading Research Quarterly, 20*(2), 233–253.

National Reading Panel. (2000). *Teaching children to read: An evidence-based assessment of the scientific research literature on reading and its implications for reading instruction. Report of the subgroups.* Washington, DC: National Institute of Child Health and Human Development. 2-93, 2-96-97.

Pinnell, G. S., & Fountas, I. (1998). *Word matters: Teaching phonics and spelling in the reading and writing classroom.* Portsmouth, NH: Heinemann.

Pressley, M. (2002). *Reading instruction that works, the case for balanced teaching.* New York: The Guilford Press.

Purcell-Gates, V. (1998). Growing successful readers: Homes, communities, and schools. In J. Osborn and F. Lehr, (Eds.), *Literacy for all: Issues in teaching and learning* (pp. 51–72). New York: Guilford Press.

Raphael, T., Highfield, K., & Au, K. (2006). *QAR: A powerful and practical framework that develops comprehension and higher level thinking in all students.* New York: Scholastic.

Rasinski, T. (2003). *The fluent reader.* New York: Scholastic.

Rathman, P. (1991). *Ruby the Copycat.* New York: Scholastic.

Rathman, P. (1995). *Officer Buckle and Gloria.* New York: Scholastic.

Richardson, V. (1990). Significant and worthwhile change in teaching practice. *Educational Researcher, 19*(7), 10–18.

Robbins, C., & Ehri, L. (1994). Reading storybooks to kindergartners helps them learn new vocabulary words. *Journal of Educational Psychology, 86,* 54–64.

Robertson, C., & Salter, W. (1997). *The phonological awareness kit: Intermediate.* East Moline, IL: LinguiSystems, Inc.

Schon, D. (1983). *The reflective practitioner: How professionals think in action.* New York: Basic Books.

Schon, D. (1987). *Educating the reflective practitioner.* San Francisco: Jossey-Bass.

Senachal, M., & Cornell, E. H. (1993). Vocabulary acquisition through shared reading experiences. *Reading Research Quarterly, 28,* 360–374.

Sindelar, P., Monda, L., & O'Shea, L. (1990). Effects of repeated reading on instructional- and mastery-level readers. *Journal of Educational Research, 83,* 220–226.

Snow, C., Barnes, W., Chandler, J., Goodman, I., & Hemphill, L. (1991). *Unfulfilled expectations: Home and school influences on literacy.* Cambridge, MA: Harvard University Press.

Snow, C., & Ninio, A. (1986). The contracts of literacy: What children learn from learning to read books. In W. Teale & E. Sulsby (Eds.), *Emergent literacy: Writing and reading* (pp. 116–138). Norwood, NJ: Ablex.

SRA/McGraw-Hill. (1999). *Corrective reading.* Monterey, CA: CTB/McGraw-Hill.

Stahl, S. (1999). *Vocabulary development.* Newton Upper Falls, MA: Brookline Books.

Stahl, S., & Fairbanks, M. (1986). The effects of vocabulary instruction: A model-based meta-analysis. *Review of Educational Research, 56,* 72–110.

Stanovich, K. (1986). Matthew effects in reading: Some consequences of individual differences in the acquisition of literacy. *Reading Research Quarterly, 21,* 360–407.

Torgesen, J. (1998). Catch them before they fall: Identification and assessment to prevent reading failure in young children. *American Educator, 22,* 32–39.

Torgesen, J. (2000). Individual differences in response to early interventions in reading: The lingering problem of treatment resisters. *Learning Disabilities Research and Practice, 15*(1), 55–64.

Torgesen, J. K., & Mathes, P. G. (1998). All children can learn to read: Critical care for the prevention of reading failure. *Peabody Journal of Education, 73*(3 & 4), 317–340.

Vygotsky, L. (1978). *Mind in society: The development of higher-level psychological processes.* Cambridge, MA: Harvard University Press.

Wagner, R., Torgesen, J., & Rashotte, C. (2001). *Comprehensive test of phonological processing.* Austin, TX: Pro-Ed.

White, T. G., Sowell, J., & Yanagihara, A. (1989). Teaching elementary students to use word-part clues. *The Reading Teacher, 42,* 302–308.

Wolf, M., & Bowers, P. (2000). The question of naming-speed deficits in developmental reading disability: An introduction to the double-deficit hypothesis. *Journal of Learning Disabilities, 33,* 322–324.

Wolf, M., & Katzir-Cohen, T. (2001). Reading fluency and its intervention. *Scientific Studies of Reading, 5,* 211–239.

Woodcock, R., Mather, N., & Schrank, F. (2006). *Woodcock-Johnson Diagnostic Reading Battery,* 3rd. Ed. (W-J III DRB). Rolling Meadows, IL: Riverside.

Worthy, J., & Broaddus, K. (2002). Fluency beyond the primary grades: From group performance to silent, independent reading. *The Reading Teacher, 55,* 334–343.

Yin, R. K. (2003). *Case study research: Design and methods.* Thousand Oaks, CA: Sage.

Yopp, H. K. (1995). A test for assessing phonemic awareness in young children. *The Reading Teacher, 49*(1), 20–29.

Index

**CORWIN
PRESS**

The Corwin Press logo—a raven striding across an open book—represents the union of courage and learning. Corwin Press is committed to improving education for all learners by publishing books and other professional development resources for those serving the field of PreK–12 education. By providing practical, hands-on materials, Corwin Press continues to carry out the promise of its motto: **"Helping Educators Do Their Work Better."**